# CHINA IN MOTION

# CHINA IN MOTION

## 17 Secrets to Slashing the Time to

- Production
- Market
- Profits

## in China, Japan and South Korea

MIA DOUCET

Bankerman Press

---

**Library and Archives Canada Cataloguing in Publication**

Doucet, Mia
China in motion: 17 secrets to slashing the time to production, to market and to profits in China, Japan and South Korea / Mia Doucet.

Includes bibliographical references and index.

ISBN 0-9735409-0-7

1. Corporate culture—East Asia. 2. Business etiquette—East Asia.

I. Title.

HF3837.D68 2004 395.5′2′095
C2004-905604-2

Published by Bankerman Press.
Printed in Canada.

First Edition

---

Book design: Fortunato Design Inc.

For my children,
who give my life deeper meaning:
Trevor, Andrés and Aimée

# Table of Contents

## PART II: BUSINESS PROTOCOL



## APPENDICES

## ILLUSTRATIONS

# How to Get the Most from This Book

Consider this book your one-source reference to working with Asians on location or from your office.

**Index:** Using this book is easy. If you have a specific enquiry, go to the Index.

**Part I:** The Secrets in Part I stand alone and can be read in any sequence and still make sense. Unless you are involved in negotiations, you are unlikely to need to read them all. Consider them required reading if you are.

If you want a deeper understanding of the differences in the mindsets of East and West, start with Secret #1. Once you understand how Asians define trust, everything falls into place.

**Part II:** This section deals with the practicalities of business and social etiquette, to smooth the work relationship.

**Appendices:** It's always tempting to ignore the appendices. But you will find them full of practical information. If you are an entrepreneur, you will find Appendix V and Appendix VI invaluable for securing business in China. If you travel to China, your survival tools include a map, embassy contacts, a karaoke songbook to endear you to older Asians—even tips for negotiating with street vendors.

# Introduction

Imagine my joy, receiving a client's call from his hotel room in South Korea at 2:35 a.m., Seoul time. He had just returned from an evening of ritual drinking after signing a multi-million dollar contract.

He was tipsy enough that I was the only one he could call to celebrate. He said, "I am so *grateful* for what you taught me, Mia. When we were negotiating, they asked me, 'How do you know this?' And I said, 'I had great training.' People need this information. You really need to write a book."

This client had been doing a lot of things right. But there was one thing he had not been doing that, undetected, would have cost his company this contract and many more. That one small thing varies with every client. My hope for you is that you will find your one small thing within these pages.

I did not so much write as compile this book. It represents the insights of many, many people who allowed me to pick their brains and use their words and ideas. Constant references would just have been distracting, so I have often presented material without directly crediting the rightful sources.

CHINA IN MOTION reveals the secrets of how my clients bridge the cultural divide to make millions and millions of dollars in the fastest growing economy in the world. These 17 Secrets will change how you interact with your Asian clients, suppliers and venture partners. You will communicate more effectively with local staff. You will understand and easily compensate for the dramatic differences in culture. You will avoid costly mistakes. And you will find it much easier to form the alliances of trust that Asians so cherish.

Dealing with Asia is an art and a skill—one that is developed over time. This book provides the tools to polish this very critical skill. My focus is primarily China, with examples from Japanese and Korean culture, often indicated by the flag of the respective country.

Things are changing so rapidly, and the Chinese are so adaptable, that what is true today may not be true tomorrow. These 17 Secrets, however, are durable and abiding truths rooted in the deep structure of Chinese culture. They will provide solid grounding regardless of the pace of change.

One always risks offending people with the sorts of generalizations required to put a point across. Certainly, within any culture, people differ according to education and experience. Your best strategy is to use the following information as a backdrop for your own joys of discovery.

Since this book aims to be your most practical, trusted, up-to-date resource for doing business in Asia, I invite you to assist in keeping the material current by reporting changes as they arise. Please also tell me about your experiences in the Pacific Rim. Your story may be included in future books or editions. I can be contacted at china@chinainmotion.com. Also visit us on the web at www.chinainmotion.com.

Mia Doucet
London, Canada
September 30, 2004

# PART I:
# 17 SECRETS

# SECRET #1: Trust is Not What You Think It Is

What do sixty green garbage bags full of cold hard cash have to do with trust?

Yuan was piling up faster than the developers could bag it. It was stage one, concept phase of a $150 million gated community in Shanghai. Investors were selecting plots for their new homes from rough sketches pinned to the boardroom wall. A thousand plots for the taking, including private residences, condos and multi-housing units.

## Trust Moves Mountains

Kelvin Hutchinson, the Australian venture partner, had never seen anything like it: "The project had been approved just three weeks earlier. The elevator doors opened and I saw long lines of people, waiting to place their deposits. It was mind snapping. Truly awe-inspiring. There were already sixty bags of cash stacked against the wall. The line-up of investors disappeared around the corner and kept growing. It was pure blind faith that if they put their money down, they would get that piece of land. They *trusted* the developer.

**China**

> *"Trust is virtually purchased. You never really have the ultimate trust. It's a commercial trust."*
>
> ~ Kelvin Hutchinson, CEO, Vision in Action Pty Ltd. (Australia)

"Two weeks later, bulldozers began clearing the land—a sign to the investors that their money was being put to work. The development was completed on time and within budget. Everyone was happy. We got paid every cent we negotiated. The time frame of the development from concept to completion was almost incomprehensible from a Western perspective, because powerful people can move mountains in China."

> *"I saw so many big and small Western companies come and go in the eight years I was in Asia. They had not developed the value propositions clearly enough either for the short or longer term aspect of the deal."*
>
> ~ Kelvin Hutchinson, CEO, Vision in Action Pty Ltd. (Australia)

## "Doing Business with the Enemy"

Deals fall apart at an alarming rate in China, for lack of trust. Nowhere does the clash of cultures present itself more forcibly than in that sphere.

Yet, Chinese expatriate and importer/exporter, Yen Chung explains: "It's so hard for Chinese to trust even each other. Even if we come from the same country, it's hard to trust one another. This is all since the Cultural Revolution. It's the way they survived and now survive in the culture."

Trusting foreigners presents a challenge. Some people still refer to outsiders as *Japanese ghosts* and *Western ghosts*. Why ghosts? "Sucking Chinese business, culture, affection."

## Barbarians at the Gate

The Chinese, Japanese and Korean languages all have a word for "foreigner" that happens also to mean "barbarian." In both Japan and Korea, use of the term is now considered repugnant, backward, and in bad taste.

> *"We have different starting points. Different perspectives. That's what we have to understand about each other."*
>
> ~ JinSeung Lee, P.Eng., Applications Engineer, Motor Division, Siemens VDO Automotive Inc.

In China, which has not yet enjoyed the benefits of decades of global trading, the term persists. As one Chinese acquaintance expressed it, "We say 'barbarian' because Chinese think we have a long history, while Western people are new. They don't have the culture. [Some Chinese] take advantage of the fact that Westerners are trustworthy, because they're *just barbarians.*"

Kelvin Hutchinson observes: "They love us and they hate us. They tolerate us for the deal. You're assumed to be a barbarian until your value to them is very clearly understood, believed, and endorsed by the ultimate decision-makers. Once the trust is built, they see you as an advisor and source of knowledge, information and guidance."

Chinese still seek to maintain the advantage when dealing with foreigners. The world has taken so much from China, that some feel entitled to take back as much as they can from the "barbarians" crowding at the gates. Until you are a known quantity and there is a history between you, Chinese will view you as an outsider.

Historical roots run deep. And Chinese are cautious with good reason (see Appendix XI). Their ability to trust others was severed by centuries of betrayals, foreign occupations, civil wars, violent revolutions, and brutal power regimes. They learned to cope by relying solely on those in their intimate circle.

### Clash of Cultures

Trust is never easy, to be sure. It requires us to lower our defenses and allow ourselves to be vulnerable to another person. Trust is even more difficult across cultures, where expectations and values often conflict. A chasm exists where people trust from different levels of their being. But once you grasp what Asian trust means, and you start to do the right things, you can bridge the chasm.

**MILLION DOLLAR MISTAKE #1:**

Assuming that everyone is just like us.

In workshops, I have found it helpful to use visual models to explain that Asians and Westerners arrive at trust from totally different perspectives. The difference accounts for many of the difficulties encountered in doing business in the East.

**Figure 1.1**

Western Trust: Independence

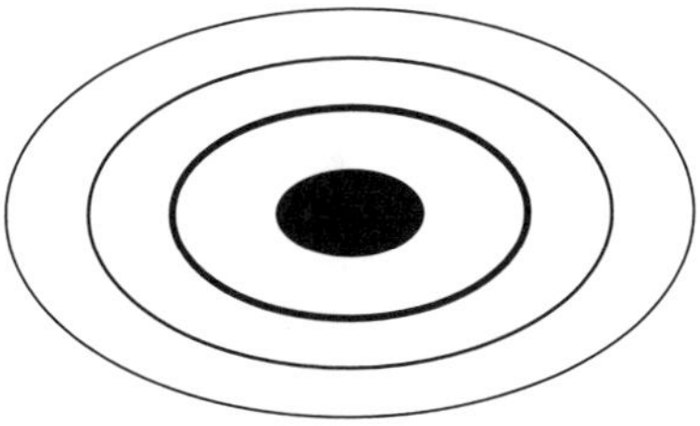

As Figure 1.1 illustrates, the Westerner's thick inner core represents a strong, individual sense of self. The outer protective layers are rather thin because the sense of self is already well-protected.

The outermost layer represents the face Westerners present to strangers. This wall of (usually) polite reserve and impersonality falls away pretty quickly. A smile, a handshake, and an exchange of first names in a business meeting is usually all that it takes to get to a level of friendliness and trust. Protected at the heart, a person is free to engage at more superficial levels of relationship.

Most business relationships are formed and remain at this level of easy camaraderie. This explains why Chinese view Westerners as "naïve and trustworthy." The trust is easy to obtain. It requires no depth, no sense of connection.

> *"Chinese see Westerners as naïve and trustworthy."*
> ~ Chinese Entrepreneur

In part, Westerners are able to trust people from this place, without deep personal involvement because of the protection of "rule of law." They mitigate risks through written contracts as opposed to having to trust at a deep level.

Clients say that although trust is easy to establish in Western cultures, there is a down side: the loyalty is not there. You can lose the relationship easily. Something goes wrong and your customer threatens to go to the competition. So it takes a lot of energy to maintain a trusting relationship.

**Figure 1.2**

Eastern Trust:
Mutual Dependence

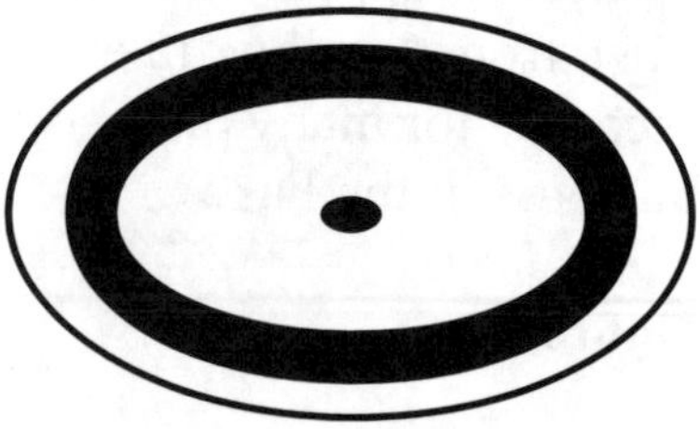

By contrast, the small inner core of the Eastern model (Figure 1.2) represents the idea that the self is small and one is not as important as the group. Asians draw their identity not from *self*-concept but from *group* connectedness. A sense of security derives from these close connections. People in one's inner circle depend and rely on one another unconditionally. And where "rule of man" substitutes for "rule of law," one needs the protection of a close network of friends.

> *"Within their own families and their own closed circle, they are trusting and trustworthy. But if you're not in the circle, don't even try. Keep some distance. It's respect for Chinese to keep some distance."*
>
> ~YEN CHUNG, IMPORTER/EXPORTER

Trust comes from the core. This vulnerability requires protection from those who are outside one's inner circle. That is the role of the thick protective crust or layer—to protect against outsiders.

The public persona of the outer layer also forms an effective barrier to establishing the business relationship. It masks personal motives and renders the Asian hard to read and almost impossible to get to know. Western businesspeople will experience this "mask" as serious and gracious, polite and implacable. You are not seeing the *person*. You are seeing surface behaviors that in Asian cultures are required to maintain harmony and save face at all times. This façade often proves confusing to the Westerner. And misreading the façade proves costly.

> *"When people use the word 'friend' with Asians, I laugh. To the Asian, the definition of 'friend' is someone who would risk their life or their fortune for you, or both. It goes back to obligations."*
>
> ~ HAROLD WONG, PHD, BERKELEY UNIVERSITY OF CALIFORNIA

With the Easterner, you have to go through a long, formal process. But once the Asian makes the decision to have a business relationship, there is deep engagement of a kind rarely found in Western business. As a Chinese businessperson said to me, "Once I trust you, I identify with you. You become part of my inner circle. You help define who I am. Does it not make sense then that I am

*"With Westerners, you may get trust easily, but in the end, they're not as loyal. (Customer name) has given us hundreds of millions of dollars of business, and still I don't get to the core with her. I know nothing about her family, for example. With Asians, I get to a deeper relationship."*

~ NAME WITHHELD, NORTH AMERICAN AUTOMOTIVE CLIENT

*"Even in men, there is that deep sense of the maternal looking after. You can count on your mother to always do what is in your best interests."*

~ NATE IIKUBO, ADVANCE PURCHASING, JAPANESE AUTOMOTIVE TIER 1 FIRM (DETROIT, MICHIGAN, USA)

going to keep you at bay until sufficient time has passed between us that I know I can rely on you from the core of my being?"

### Asian Trust and *Dependent Love*

There is a word unique to Asian cultures (*ai* in China; in Japan, it is *amae*; in Korea, *sarang*) that describes a deep, loving, and dependent connection to mother. That same connection and sense of dependency extend to relatives, spouses, dear and trusted friends, classmates, and business colleagues. Without a Western word equivalent, nothing prepares us for this cultural rarity. The closest translation—*dependent love*—explains the Asian's deep vulnerability. It also explains many things that baffle the Westerner: why the relationship is more important than the business deal and cannot be rushed; why promises are sacred; commitment to the collective good; the depth of trust and reliance on suppliers; the need to share risks (often at the expense of profit).

### Impact on Supplier Relationships: Trust Through Thick and Thin

When the relationship of trust has been entered into, one is expected to do the right thing, whatever the cost. You do your service—when times are good and when times are down. There is no question of bailing out. You must demonstrate your willingness and ability to stick it through for your Asian partner, to be judged trustworthy. A strong bond is established. When a similar situation arises, you will likewise be able to count on them because of that bond.

My Asian sources tell me that with North American companies, there is a tendency to want to bail when times are tough. Asian companies want to deal with suppliers who understand both risk sharing and growing together. As one Japanese-American put it: "I need to be able to count on you if things get tough, just as I can count on mother."

> *"We create long-term agreements, but North Americans want to leave the long-term agreements open so they can get out of them. They have a clause that says if your prices aren't competitive, if at any time in the three-year contract we feel we can get it cheaper elsewhere, we want you to match that price. Asians take exception to that. In their eyes, that is not a partnership."*
>
> ~ Brent D. Moorcroft, General Manager, Power Train Management Business Unit, Johnson Electric (Hong Kong)

### Inroads to Trust

There are ways to gain traction, even as an outsider, to enter the circle of trust. Unfortunately, there is no fast track. What does it take? Time. Persistence. Patience and humility. Generosity. Transparency. Strong communication (written, visual, timely). Long-term thinking. Sharing of risk. Focus on relationship over business. Willingness to document in detail. A sophisticated, detached approach. A relationship of equals: neither side takes advantage of the other; each does what is best for both. You do everything you can to build trust while taking precautions.

When you work for a global firm, your relationship with the entire organization, including the contact level, is extremely important. Get to know people in the plant. It is key because Asian managers rely so heavily on input from their subordinates.

If you are an entrepreneur, it is essential that you prepare your intermediary for meetings with Buddha, the Patriarch, Matriarch—whoever the powerful person is who can move mountains. (See Appendix VI for your roadmap to building trust through Working Papers.)

*"With Easterners, there's more of an expectation that you will be part of a business they are involved in. You cannot really say no, once you have developed a relationship. You're in for the whole deal. They want me to be in Asia next week, again. I cannot say no to them because of the relationship. How can I think of not going?"*

~ JOE VARGHESE,
CUSTOMER PROJECTS MANAGER,
MOTOR DIVISION,
SIEMENS AUTOMOTIVE INC.

## Genuine Connection

You have to establish a history for yourself and your company. Think of trust as an upward spiral that builds over time. The cycle of trust is always being built up or torn down. The cycle repeats with each project and every interaction.

Always assume you are starting at the first stage in the cycle, respectfully presenting yourself into the relationship again after any absence, acknowledging past business, always quietly reinforcing the bond.

Asian companies complain that once North American companies win the business, they disappear: "You never see management again." Make sure your senior executives are available in person to review the business. If you are in sales or management, rebuild the relationship at least once every quarter.

The process takes a long, long time by Western standards and cannot be rushed. Invest the time and go to the expense of nurturing the relationship regularly. Once established, you will know the meaning of trust.

***Trust Quick Tips:***

- ✓ Every morning, ask yourself, "What one specific thing can I do today to build trust?"
- ✓ Schedule regular face-to-face visits with your Asian customer.
- ✓ Call your major customers and let them know if you will be away from your office for any period of time.

# SECRET #2:
# To the Chinese Mind, an Idea is Not Something You Can Own or Sell

A comment by a Chinese expatriate caused me to rethink my point of view regarding the sensitive issue of intellectual property rights in China. We were in a seminar, discussing communication with Asians. I mentioned my global clients' concerns over the lack of patent protection in China. Without legal means to protect its ideas and technologies, a company could find itself out of profits, out of competition, and out of existence.

This educated, thoughtful, sophisticated engineer responded by saying, "How can a person own an idea? More important than ownership is that large numbers of people make a living from the idea." Fascinating! Why would you refuse to share a document or design that could bring good fortune to many people? How could a Western company, claiming long-term commitment to China, put a price on technology that could benefit the entire country?

**China**

In China, ideas are like air. Would you ask a Westerner to pay for air?

## One Bowl of Rice, Five Eaters

The "You will not be hungry" mindset is one of the reasons behind the lavish banquets favored by Chinese.

As my colleague explained, the overriding sentiment in her home country has always been: "You will not be hungry. You will have enough food." This mindset evolved from centuries of widespread poverty. A survival strategy emerged of individuals linking their fates to an inner circle of friends and family. By sharing scarce resources, the group stood a better chance of survival.

The fact that consulting is a booming industry in China seems to be one indication that things are changing. However, much Chinese "consulting" is based upon reciprocal obligations (Secret #4), a traditional way of doing business that has little to do with an exchange of intellectual expertise.

*"The Business Software Alliance, a nonprofit trade group, estimates that as much as 95 percent of all software in China is pirated, though the industry hopes China's expected admission to the World Trade Organization will change that."*

~ CRAIG S. SMITH, THE NEW YORK TIMES, JULY 7, 2000 [1]

Within this circle, there was no question of hoarding. There was no question of individual claim over even the smallest bowl of rice.

That cultural pattern persists today. Now the group wants to share an idea as it once shared a bowl of rice. Technology is the new scarce resource. Those of us who have always had our own bowl of rice cannot comprehend that this way of thinking could so permeate everyday business life in China.

This mindset accounts for the behavior described by Roland Bauer, Vice President and General Manager, Siemens VDO Automotive Inc. (Germany): "In China, if the customer asks for something, the local staff will deliver. We say, 'Let's look at this from three or four sides, work out the pros and cons.' But our Asian colleagues are more willing to give the customer anything they want: cost breakdowns, technical content, samples, company secrets."

It explains why no stigma attaches to software piracy and intellectual property infringement. In the words of a Chinese engineer: "If I have the ability to learn it, it belongs to me now. We don't think it's so serious to copy. Other people won't look down on you if you copy."

Of course, this attitude will change due to international pressures. In joining the World Trade Organization in 2001, China promised to do away with intellectual property theft. But until that time comes, you still have the challenge of protecting your intellectual assets.

## Paranoid, Who's Paranoid?

Once you understand the thought process, you can build a strategy that in one stroke respects people's dignity, protects your intellectual assets and creates loyalty. The fact that this will result in decreased turnover is a huge added bonus.

**MILLION DOLLAR MISTAKE #2:**

Not taking the necessary precautions to protect your idea.

## Policy

*Strategic*

Remove the opportunity for theft at the source:

- Design and store your intellectual property offshore.
- Keep the component parts in various global locations.
- Register trademarks and patents immediately.
- Design your products such that they cannot easily be duplicated.

*"Reverse engineering is easy. As the Japanese found out 50 years ago, you can get any American to spill his guts by assigning him a 'quote' consulting contract for $100,000 or $200,000. He'll spill his guts and give up trade secrets on an R&D process that took a hundred million dollars and 10 years to develop. If you look at this as economic warfare, that American should be tried for treason."*

~ Harold Wong, PhD, Berkeley University of California

*Basic Lock and Key*

Educate anyone who has access to highly confidential information about the potential risk of intellectual property theft. Take the same precautions as you would anywhere else in the world:

- Keep track of telephone costs on your fax lines and secure all fax retrievals.
- Do not leave important documents lying around for all to see.
- Review all information before forwarding, with the thought in mind that it will be distributed.
- Monitor careless conversation.
- Lock office doors and drawers.
- Change the password security on your computer network and alarms regularly.

**MILLION DOLLAR MISTAKE #3:**

Not getting cross-cultural training for Chinese local staff.

*Cross-Cultural Business Training*

Provide training programs to your Chinese employees in Western business practices. Talk to them about the protection of intellectual assets in a way that is meaningful within the Chinese context. Let them know that, as a group, protecting your competitive advantage is how they can ensure the company's longevity and how they can contribute to their country's growth in wealth and international prestige and respect.

*Hiring*

Hire people right out of school so that you can instill your company's values rather than inherit work practices that do not align with yours. Ensure that your employees are well paid by local standards.

Hire competent women. The consensus among Westerners who teach in China is that they are more focused, work harder, work longer hours, and are more ready to please than their male counterparts. Women are often over-looked for all the reasons they once were in Western culture. Those reasons were not valid then, and they are not valid now.

**QUICK TIP:**

Make your expectations crystal clear and provide positive reinforcement for desired behaviors. In China, that means cash.

Have everyone sign confidentiality agreements.

Finally, your HR strategy needs to include a plan that allows everyone to save face, in case a Chinese manager seeks to place an unqualified friend or relative in an important position in your joint venture.

*Create an Inner Circle*

Skip the pep talk on profit and productivity. Position your company as an integral part of their vision for China's future. Build on the profound Asian need for belonging to a close inner circle, where personal connection, mutual trust, and the ability to depend on one another unquestioningly guarantees survival. Come through for your people when they need you most. Expect to spend more time on employee relationships than required in the West. You may need to micromanage for a while. Get to know your staff and colleagues on a personal basis. Take an interest in their families.

In time, your efforts will engender the deep Asian loyalty that Japanese and Korean companies enjoy. A loyalty that would never permit sharing company secrets with outsiders.

**MILLION DOLLAR MISTAKE #4:**

*Running your operation as if it was a North American operation; upsetting your native Chinese managers who then in turn quit and start a competing operation.*

~ Gerry Murak, Turnaround Performance Specialist

# SECRET #3: Everything is Relative, Including Truth

One of my automotive clients was invited to bid on a major contract with a global OEM customer in Japan. They were already working on a project together. As part of the bid process, his company was asked to benchmark its own product against the competition. "We were told, 'Tell us everything, and tell us the truth.' We thought that was comical, because we normally do tell the truth. In hindsight, I think maybe what they wanted was the truth about the good things. We lost the contract to an Asian firm."

My client asked whether there was anything that could have changed this unforeseen turn of fortune. He received an apologetic email response from his engineering counterpart in Asia, confiding he had been "too honest" and "should not have told us everything, especially bad news. Never provide that kind of bad news before the sourcing—or even after the sourcing." Then he ended with a bit of Asian wisdom: "I think it is better to be careful from now on. Silence is a virtue."

## High-Context Communication

As my client discovered, in the deep structure of Asian culture there is always more going on than meets the eye. The meaning of a communication depends on the larger context. Communication is far deeper than words, and often does not involve words.

Moreover, words are often used to placate and smooth things over to guarantee surface harmony (Secret #6). Therefore, words may have little relationship to the true intent. Given the choice between telling a truth that risks giving offense, or telling an outright lie, Asians will be vague and ambiguous. Sins of omission are acceptable for ensuring that relationships are harmonious. (This means that the Western tendency to question is often misinterpreted as rude or an open challenge to the other person's dignity and integrity.)

### High-Context Culture

Everything connects to everything else and has to be considered within a larger framework. A thing only makes sense when viewed within its full context. Nothing stands alone. There's no such thing as an isolated fact.

**MILLION DOLLAR MISTAKE #5:**

Forgetting that in a high-context culture everything connects to everything.

### Truth is Subjective

This sheds light on why truth is not absolute in Eastern cultures like it is in Western cultures. It depends on the larger context, not just the matter at hand. This context includes the people involved, their past history (including existing mutual obligations), and the long-term implications of any decision on those relationships.

And if circumstances change, or time passes, or different people become involved, what is true may change as well. The shifting nature of truth explains the "conditional ethics" of Asian culture. We may not see the full picture.

Although my client's company lost the contract, the story ended happily. Their existing work relationship with the OEM greatly improved. Why? Because now they could be trusted to tell the truth. In the larger context of the relationship, this was the more desirable outcome, because it opened the way to more contracts in the future.

### Making the Connections

More mental preparation and flexibility in communication are required on the part of the Westerner in order to engage at a deeper level where trust can take hold.

*1. When Assessing a Situation:*

Always consider the various (often invisible) component parts that can affect the outcome of a situation. Perhaps the best way to do this is through a series of questions, some of which are best answered with the assistance of your interpreter.

*Ask:*

- How does this transaction fit into the bigger picture? What events preceded it?
- Is it good for all parties? How does it affect the collective good?
- Will this be seen as right for the long-term?
- Am I too focused on the moment?
- Who are the other people involved? Have I considered the full impact of the transaction on them?
- Do mutual obligations exist that might affect the outcome?
- What is the history of our relationship? How deep is the trust?

*2. In Conversation:*

Take more time to clarify the communication to make sure everyone has the same picture in mind. Be prepared to talk around a topic until you are sure you have reached a mutual understanding. Consider everything that is said in the light of the bigger picture and the full context.

*Ask:*

- Have I understood the full communication? Have I made the mistake of thinking that my words have been clearly understood?
- What, if anything, has been sacrificed to surface harmony? What am I missing?
- Is there potential for anyone to lose face? How can that be avoided?
- What should be left unsaid? What may need to be compromised in order to preserve this relationship?

# SECRET #4:
# Think in Terms of a Web of Relationships

Westerners like to feel that we are responsible for our own success. "It's not what you know, but who you know" offends many of us. In truth, we may not like it so much when it accrues to the benefit of others, but do not mind when it opens doors for ourselves and loved ones. That's human nature. It goes on in every culture—subtly or otherwise.

We all have a network, but again Western and Asian models are quite distinct. Your own network likely consists of respected colleagues with whom you interact, share ideas and enjoy camaraderie. You come together to work on a project or carry out a transaction, and when the project is completed, go your separate ways. Connections are made, they serve their purpose for the moment, and they pass. New connections are made. Rarely do the connections and relationships you cultivate in the West form future obligations.

In Asian cultures, getting things done through a complex network of social transactions is a venerated, 4,000-year-old tradition. It is central to the culture and encompasses all the values described throughout the 17 Secrets. The networks now extend across the globe.

For thousands of years, Chinese were taught they could only fulfill themselves by fulfilling the needs of others—the

*"Japanese have to look out for the collective interest of the society. It's a cultural characteristic. If you didn't stay together as a group, if you didn't have a well-established sense of community, your survival was at stake."*

~ Nate Iikubo, Advance Purchasing, Japanese automotive Tier 1 firm (Detroit, Michigan, USA)

*"There was a nation-wide discussion in many of the major newspapers in the early eighties asking if seeking self-value (namely, personal success) is morally correct. And believe it or not, the conclusion (by government-owned newspapers) was negative."*

~ Calvin Wang, Product Engineer, Power Train Group, Siemens VDO Automotive Inc.

nation, society and the family. This belief is still held dear by the older generation. But even among the younger crowd, the network of interpersonal relationships remains as important as the surfacing desire for independence.

### No Relationship, No Business

**China**

*"For the new generation of Chinese, independence and a network of interpersonal relationships have equal importance."*

~ JUN LU, ME, P. ENG., APPLICATIONS ENGINEER, MOTOR DIVISION, SIEMENS VDO AUTOMOTIVE INC.

On your own, you will find it impossible to get ahead in China. You have to align yourself with someone who has the personal connections or *guanxi* (pronounced *kwan shee*).

The *guanxi* relationship extends beyond the simple exchange of favors between two people. *Guanxi* is a form of currency that can be amassed and exchanged. One does the other a favor. This creates a tacit obligation for the other person to reciprocate at a later date. Years may go by and the obligation stands. The one trusts that the other will come through when the occasion demands. Failure to do so would result in loss of *mianzi*—or face (discussed in Secret #6).

### Friends in High Places

The better one's *guanxi*—the more complex the web—the more valuable this social asset is. The quality of one's connections is also important. The more powerful they are, the better educated, the greater their connections, the wealthier and the more popular—the greater their status. And the greater their capacity to obtain favors from others and to positively control outcomes.

### A Network of Favors

*Guanxiwang* describes a complex network of interlinking exchanges or transactions that occur when other parties become involved. Person A owes an obligation to Person

B, and fulfills that obligation through Person C (or D, E, F, and beyond). The system sustains itself through reciprocity. There has to be mutual benefit to both parties. Reciprocity requires that all parties contribute to and protect each others' face and prestige.

### Is *Guanxiwang* Corrupt?

The impact of corruption on Chinese business is well documented. Our first response, then, may be to attach a negative connotation to this ancient custom. Instead, think of it as a neutral constant. The practice exists. It has existed for centuries and is not likely to go away any time soon. The system becomes corrupt only when it involves illegal transactions. In fact, a *guanxiwang* based on trust can be a protection against corruption.

> *"In guanxiwang, Chinese trust each other at least a little bit. It is within that framework that they are willing to take some risk."*
> ~ Yen Chung, Importer/Exporter

Until you have cultivated your own trusted network of local contacts, you will gain competitive advantage through a reliable partner's *guanxi*. You want someone whose business network includes local, regional, and national government connections (particularly local city governments, since that is where the real power lies).

### Who is Owed a Favor?

Bearing this in mind, the web forms a network of mutual obligations that may have serious consequences for your business now and in future. With the high turnover rate in China, many Western-based companies are concerned about the loss of their intellectual property when people leave the firm. But the larger concern may be with those who stay. Employees on payroll could be forwarding your company secrets.

> *"In the West, we network to help each other without any expectation of a return. Whereas in Asia, there's a hidden agenda and that is what Westerners find difficult to grapple with."*
> ~ Kelvin Hutchinson, CEO, Vision in Action Pty Ltd. (Australia)

Do you know the obligations others may be incurring on your behalf? In this system, favors always have to be repaid, in one form or another. Nothing comes for free. Sooner or later, you will find you are expected to reciprocate in kind. Failure to do so will cause loss of face and could have a negative impact on your business. So the loyalty of your managers, your staff, your suppliers, venture partners, and interpreters is critical. (For more discussion on *guanxi* and the role of your interpreter, see Secret #5.)

**Remember the Inner Circle**

Remember that there are many barriers to building trust in accessing the inner circle. Generally, Asians are wary of outsiders, so they tend to not want to involve themselves personally with strangers outside their web of personal connections. The only way to break into their circle is through a personal introduction. Approaching directly, without an introduction, is bad business. In Japan and Korea, it is considered rude. At the very least, it arouses suspicion. In entrepreneurial China, it may not be considered rude, but you won't get where you want to go.

The initial introduction must be made by a business associate who is trusted and held in high esteem by the other party, because that esteem and trust transfer to you. The person's rank and status also transfer to you and your company. The higher the status of the person who makes the introduction—the higher the esteem in which that person is held—the stronger your position.

**QUICK TIP:**

Approach any new contact through a personal introduction.

*"Always spend the time to have the most powerful third party that you can to make the introduction, because you are leveraging their credibility. The more powerful the intermediary, the more powerful a relationship you will have."*

~ Kelvin Hutchinson, CEO, Vision in Action Pty Ltd. (Australia)

Furthermore, the person who introduces you takes on responsibility for your character and your actions. So you need to take great care to never do anything to undermine their reputation and relationships.

**MILLION DOLLAR MISTAKE #6:**

Not making commitments Asians can count on.

# SECRET #5:

# A Trusted, Well-Connected, Savvy Liaison is Critical to Your Success

**China**

If you are an entrepreneur seeking to establish a foothold for your venture in China, see also Appendix V.

Having your own liaison will mitigate the risk of doing business in China. Do not try to go it alone. The person will be indispensable at smoothing the gap between two languages, cultures and worldviews. If your company already employs a Chinese interpreter, use the person's expertise to the fullest extent to open doors and protect you from yourself. Take good care of this relationship. If you already have such a liaison, you do not need the rest of this chapter. Save your time and skip the next few pages.

If, on the other hand, you are depending on a translator or interpreter provided by your JV partner, embassy, or government contact to represent you in China, or you are sharing an interpreter, you may be making a serious tactical mistake. Read on.

### Hire at Home

You want to hire your liaison on your home turf, rather than waiting to find someone in Asia. This is much easier and far more reliable. Start your search through your Chinese embassy. Contact Western teachers of English at Chinese universities. Make inquiries at a Western graduate business school that attracts mature expatriate students to its programs.

**QUICK TIP:**

Treat your liaison very, very well.

This is no time to be bargain hunting. Your liaison will make or break the deal overseas. My clients' average contract is worth $10 million. Over three years, that's $30 million on one contract alone.

Is it not worth investing the time and money to find and attract the right person?

## 12 Qualities of the Ideal *Zhongjian Ren* (Interpreter)

1. He or she is a Chinese expatriate who has work experience in both the East and the West.
2. Preferably, emigrated within the past five years (because China is changing so rapidly).
3. Speaks fluent English and fluent Mandarin, if you are working in Mainland China and Taiwan, or Cantonese, if in Hong Kong. But more than a translator of words, you want someone who can interpret culture. You want someone whose speaking ability matches his or her comprehension.
4. Has an active network of business relationships (*guanxi*) so that you are not starting from scratch. This allows you to break into business circles and the inner sanctum of trust with proper introductions. (Even if they do not have the contacts, it will be easier for them to establish than for you.) The network should include both government and business contacts.
5. Knows the local Chinese bureaucracy and their laws. Able to speed the bureaucratic process through connections (*guanxi)* with government leadership and business sectors.
6. Willing to make introductions to help you establish your own *guanxi*.
7. Has the versatility to be direct and to-the-point with you to satisfy your need for the unvarnished truth, while at the same time satisfying the Asian need for respect, face and surface harmony.
8. Understands your industry, including its trends, challenges and specialized terminology.
9. Will be loyal to the goals and interests of your company and will negotiate on your behalf.

10. Appreciates and can speak to the advantages of Western technology, quality, management and administration.
11. Demonstrates the ability to adapt communication to what the situation requires. This goes beyond bilingual fluency and familiarity with up-to-the-minute industry jargon. It means the person has the objectivity to interpret nuance and clarify ambiguities.
12. Finally, and importantly, is capable of handling the inevitable conflicts that will arise in the clash of business cultures without losing face and without caving in to the Chinese side.

**QUICK TIP:**

Due to the cultural complexities of communication, you want an interpreter, and not just a translator. There is a difference in skill level and remuneration.

### *Guanxi* Caution

What you don't want is to hire someone who was referred to you through guanxi and not put through a rigorous selection process. Do take care to determine that this network will not result in obligations being owed to the wrong people. Do you know where your liaison's loyalties lie? Is your liaison trustworthy? Will he or she be willing to safeguard your interests above Chinese interests?

**QUICK TIP:**

Check an interpreter's qualifications through International Translators Associations.

### Selection Process

Include questions and scenarios that both reveal the person's thought process and show how they would behave in a situation. Make the questions different enough that the candidate cannot prepare for the interview through expert coaching. A prolonged conversation will reveal the level of language comprehension.

*Questions:*

1. What business network do you have in China?
2. Who can you contact? What can you tell me about that person?
3. How would you propose representing our interests in China?
4. In your opinion, what is the biggest mistake Westerners make when communicating with Asians?
5. In your experience, what are the differences between Western and Chinese business culture and practices? What can one learn from the other?

*Scenarios:*

1. Tell me how you would handle this (compromising) situation: You are part of a joint venture. A conflict of interest arises between the parties on the issue of quality control. You are viewed as representing foreign interests. How do you make your decision as to how to conduct yourself?
2. The General Manager of a Coca-Cola Joint Venture Partnership questioned why both a driver and a salesperson were required to make product deliveries. Why did they need two people to do the job that one could do? It proved to be a major issue. In the end, the GM lost his battle for efficiency: they retained both the driver and the salesperson. Why do you suppose this happened? Is it because Chinese fight efficiency and productivity?

*Note:* The question gets at the cultural issue of face. If you tell people you work as a salesperson, people will show respect. If you say you drive a truck, then you're just blue-collar. (Interestingly, that's the term used in China.) Coca-Cola was unable to resolve this cultural issue. Your liaison ought to be able to tell you which battles you can win, and which will take another twenty years.

### How to Work with Your Interpreter

- Give your interpreter permission to tell you when you are off track.
- Brief the person at every stage of your meeting preparation.
- Speak in complete sentences. Keep them short. Pause frequently.
- Don't complicate life by throwing in humor. It doesn't translate.

**MILLION DOLLAR MISTAKE #7:**

Not using a go-between to build initial trust. Not using a totally trustworthy go-between who will protect you from yourself.

A *zhongjian ren* is more than a translator. A *zhongjian ren* is someone through whom you will have access to local knowledge and inside information. Someone who can lead you to the real decision-maker. Someone who will help you cut through bureaucratic red tape and move mountains so that approval processes move along more quickly. Someone with access to reliable local suppliers who will provide product at a fraction of your present cost and ensure a smoother transportation of goods.

One of the services he or she can perform for you is to interpret exactly what your Asian customer wants: What are the challenges? What keeps them awake at night? What drives them? In what ways have they been stung in the past by foreigners? What concerns do they have that are not being addressed?

In addition, in the absence of a sound legal system, you want someone who will help you collect monies owed. And—at the extreme—ensure retribution on your behalf if patent laws are broken. A very tall order indeed.

# SECRET #6:
# Understand the Concepts of "Face" and Surface Harmony

You were graciously received at the airport and treated to a sumptuous banquet, with bows and smiles and toasts. You have every reason to believe your technical presentation went well. People were polite, nodding. No objections were raised. When you asked for a response, the leader said, "It is certainly worth thinking about." You left, and everyone was gracious and polite. Now, weeks later, you are in the boardroom having to explain the lack of progress on your project. What went wrong? Why the continued delay? You have been wasting your time. You have no hope of completing on time. You feel deceived.

I know an expatriate manager who prides himself on involving his team. He confesses his frustration with Chinese managers who report directly to him: "In North America, all my managers have their chance to say their piece. Here, I say, 'You can say anything you want in these meetings. If you don't agree with me, say so. Don't sit here and nod.' But they sit there and nod."

He concludes: "I don't know how my managers got through engineering school. They're such quiet people. They don't flow out with new ideas or new outlooks on things."

This is a typical scenario that plays out over and over again with Asian customers, suppliers and local staff. Too often, Westerners misread communication cues and, as a result, judge their Asian colleagues harshly.

The confusion we feel is due in large part to two deeply rooted Asian practices: surface harmony and face. They intertwine.

## SURFACE HARMONY

Surface harmony is all about maintaining appearances so

that things will run smoothly and not cause offense or loss of face. Lack of awareness of this time-honored tradition silently costs millions of dollars each year in delays and lost contracts.

### Passive Sabotage

The preferred Asian method of suppressing conflict and hostility is passive resistance. Think of it as smiling while dragging your feet. It is a form of quiet sabotage, an artful means of avoiding conflict and confrontation: not openly refusing to do something, but showing resistance through inactivity. Not returning messages. Failing to meet a deadline or to submit a report or to show up for an important meeting. Pretending headway is being made on a project when in fact the project is stalled. Giving lip service to a suggestion, then taking no action. Making excuses that sound plausible. Saying, "The matter is under consideration." These are all socially acceptable behaviors that satisfy the requirements of surface harmony.

> *"Sweet temper and friendliness produce money."*
> ~ Chinese saying

As Westerners, we can do our part to keep this pattern to a minimum. We have to realize the role we play in delays. When we get the relationship right, when we drop the sense of urgency and stop insisting on having things done our way, we get far greater cooperation.

## THE MANY FACETS OF FACE

Face has to do with dignity and self-respect. We all want to live with dignity. We all want to be seen in a positive light. We all want others to respect us. Different cultures, however, define the conditions and terms of respect differently.

For the Westerner, face has to do with maintaining our own pride, reputation, credibility, and self-respect. If we are skilled enough, smart enough, or successful enough, we might not care too much about others' opinions of us. That's just business. Loss of face is highly individual. It means personal failure, loss of *self*-esteem or personal pride.

For the Asian, face has everything to do with honor. It relates to one's social group, including family, colleagues, former classmates, and place of work. Face is the opposite of shame. Loss of face, as you would expect, is social. It means disrupting group harmony and bringing shame, not just to oneself but to everyone in one's circle.

So, the issue of face is much more complex in the East than in the West. It is ever present and interconnects with every aspect of business life and society.

> *"I saw on many occasions the extraordinary lengths that some Chinese entrepreneurs went through to save face and cover losses in ill-conceived projects with other Asian partners—almost to the point of bankruptcy to protect the relationship. We're taught to make mistakes. They're taught to avoid mistakes at all cost."*
>
> ~ KELVIN HUTCHINSON, CEO, VISION IN ACTION PTY LTD. (AUSTRALIA)

## Face Stress

Imagine for a moment the face pressures that your Asian counterpart encounters. Take any family, social, or work issue where you have felt pressured to conform. You must do well and make your family proud. You must never hurt or bring dishonor on yourself or anyone by word or act. You must never say what is on your mind if that might prove offensive to anyone in the room. You must never cause a colleague or subordinate to lose face, even when they are under-performing on the job. You must maintain harmony at all costs. Now multiply that by a factor of 10 and you will have a small idea of what face means in Asian cultures. Whether it's called *mianzi* (China), *kao* (Japan) or *ul gul* (Korea), it means the same thing and carries the same societal pressures.

> **QUICK TIP:**
>
> Respect the enormous pressure on your Asian colleague to conform.

## FACE LOSS

Traditionally it is wrong to disagree with people in public, or to make a show of being right when another is wrong, or to answer in the negative. You will not hear "I told you so," as it is extremely impolite to point out a mistake. And as long as no one points out a mistake, the other person may assume there are no errors. As long as we are unaware, we never find out that we offended someone or why.

Simply by being your casual Western self, there is potential to disrupt harmony and cause you or your Asian counterpart to lose face.

**QUICK TIP:**

Compliment a company or a work team, but never single out an individual to compliment.

### Let Me Count the Ways

There are countless ways to cause someone to lose face. The following list reflects some of the more popular faux pas mentioned by my Asian contacts:

1. Failing to acknowledge the senior person in the room.
2. Talking to your interpreter rather than to your Asian counterpart.
3. Using humor in a business context.
4. Challenging authority.
5. Interrupting and showing impatience.
6. Pushing for an answer before your Asian counterpart has all the data to provide a complete answer.
7. Pointing out a mistake.
8. Getting annoyed at the slow pace of decision-making.
9. Insisting on talking with a key decision-maker.
10. Demanding that someone take responsibility for a (bad) decision.
11. Presenting an idea or theory that has not been fully researched or studied beforehand.
12. Writing on the person's business card, putting it in your pocket, or otherwise not giving it due respect.

Any show of temper or hostility or childishness or arrogance or disrespect or criticism compounds the face loss. All these traits are seen as serious character flaws.

Fortunately, Asians will not hold you to the same standard that they have for each another. But things go more smoothly when you go out of your way to avoid ruffled feathers.

## BLUNDER BUFFER

One way to protect surface harmony and save face is to engage a liaison, as discussed in Secret #5. It is the job of the interpreter to act as a buffer for your inevitable social blunders. If you make a negative or controversial statement, your liaison can translate it while still observing cultural protocol. If there is no effective translation possible without giving offense, your go-between will advise you of the full impact of your statement and give you an opportunity to re-phrase or reconsider your comments.

### Supplier Face

Face affects the way problems are discussed and resolved. When there are quality problems, North American customers want their questions answered on the spot: What do you know? What are you doing to solve the problem? When is it going to be fixed? The supplier is expected to respond immediately, even if he or she doesn't have the answer. The customer expects to be acknowledged and to get an accurate estimate of the time it will take for the solution to be reached.

Don't carry these expectations into Asia. Asian suppliers will not make the call to tell you they don't have the answer yet. They will avoid the conversation and are unlikely even to send an email confirming they have received your inquiry. That is because Asians do not like to respond until they have a complete answer. *It would cause loss of face.* The reasoning goes something like this: How will you be able to trust me in the future if I give you an inaccurate response now? Likewise, they will not present an idea or theory that has not been fully researched or studied beforehand because this too can cause loss of face.

Use the same logic when the relationship is reversed and you are in the supplier position. Do not deluge your Asian contact with partial answers and frequent updates. Not only will you look unprepared to them, losing face, you will add to the time it takes to production, to market, and to profits in Asia. Acknowledge the request, apologize for the inconvenience, and then wait to provide a complete and accurate response when the facts are in.

### Company Face

Asians are regularly shocked when Westerners throw their own business card on a desk or casually hand it over during introductions. It signals a lack of respect for oneself. And when we receive an Asian's card and write on it, place it in a pocket, or toss it casually into a briefcase, we signal a lack of respect for our Asian colleagues. We cause them loss of face.

Since your business card is an extension of you, the card represents the esteem in which you hold yourself and your company. It is your image, your honor, and your identity.

Your corporate face represents the esteem in which your company is held. That regard extends to your joint venture partners and circle of business relationships. It explains why Asians prefer to do business with companies that are well-connected and enjoy a fine international reputation.

**QUICK TIP:**

Treat everyone's business card, including your own, with the utmost respect.

The protocol for the business card exchange (explained in Part II) is well worth learning if you do not want to lose corporate face.

## FACE RECOVERY

In the West, we often use strategies of attack or defensiveness to avoid or recover from loss of face. Or we may mask embarrassment with good-humored banter, humor (friendly or otherwise), sarcasm or put-downs. But these ways all contribute to greater face loss for the Asian.

Moreover, a long, long memory for loss of face is ingrained in Asian cultures. Forgive and forget is not a concept that is understood. If you cause someone to lose face, be aware that they will—one day, somehow—get their revenge. Given that feelings are easily hurt, you have to always be on the alert to not cause loss of face. Invariably, though, loss of face will result from miscommunications and cultural gaps. Therefore, acquire the knack for making amends.

*"Japanese, in general, are very apologetic people. That's the first thing you are taught when you come to North America: Use your common sense. If you're in an accident, don't say 'I'm sorry.' It could be a source of miscommunication and taken as admission of guilt."*

~ Nate Iikubo, Advance Purchasing, Japanese automotive Tier 1 firm (Detroit, Michigan, USA)

## The Asian Apology

The Asian apology has been raised to a high art. Its purpose is to avoid friction, preserve peace, and increase surface harmony. The apology may be for a real or imaginary offense. Whether or not it is sincere is neither here nor there. The ability and readiness to apologize are critical to getting along because it is so easy to take or give offense. So it is both a pre-emptive strategy and a way to recover from loss or potential loss of face.

The apology is embedded in the very language of the culture. In Japanese, "I'm sorry" (*sumimasen*) also means "thank you." In Mandarin, "I'm sorry" often substitutes for "please" or "excuse me" or "thank you." The Korean language has separate words for "thank you" and "I'm sorry" but they are used almost interchangeably. ("I'm sorry, may I use this phone?" is a form of politeness.) You get the idea. The apology is automatic and part of the conditioned thought pattern.

> "People usually say first 'I am sorry' before they actually want to ask or request something. For example, whenever they want to borrow or use something owned by somebody or ask a

direction how to get there, they say 'Sorry' first. For North Americans to say 'I am sorry' means a big thing. They don't usually speak 'I am sorry' well. In Japan or Korea, 'I am sorry' is not a serious thing. It is a normal word."

~ Yun Kim, Product Engineer, Business Development, Siemens VDO Automotive Inc.

**QUICK TIP:**

Learn to apologize, humbly and often. Say, "I'm sorry." Act a little bit humble and inferior.

### *"I Will Insult You. I Apologize."*

In sticky situations, humbly explain that you are sorry. Explain that your actions reflect your country's customs and you may, without intending, do something that offends. You do not mean to. You are unfamiliar with Asian customs. Your company's policies and practices—which you cannot arbitrarily change—make it impossible for you to conform completely to their way of doing business. (This is like saying, "I may insult you but it is out of my control, and I apologize beforehand.") Asians will readily understand this reasoning. The apology will be appreciated and accepted. Face will be restored. Harmony will prevail.

**China**

## FACE PROTECTION

### Name Face

Your Chinese colleagues do not want to lose face or cause you to lose face by stumbling over your name. You might want to consider adopting a Chinese name out of respect for their need to save face, especially if your name is hard for them to spell or pronounce.

By this act, you give yourself face, give your contacts face, and save their face in one fell swoop. It's also a fun way to build rapport.

If you choose to do so, start by going to www.mandarintools.com[2]. The site invites you to select a

Chinese name based on your English name. You enter your first and family names, gender, and birth date. Then you select the "desired essence of the name" from a field of five possibilities: personal character and skill; wealth and fortune; beauty and appearance; mind and intelligence; strength and power.

The Chinese surname has one character. It comes before the given name, which is usually composed of two characters. You will see what each of the characters means. Once you find a few combinations that you like, ask a native Chinese whether the three characters' sounds, meaning, and appearance go together and place you in a positive light.

**QUICK TIP:**

Chinese names are easily recognizable for their one-syllable surname.

That is what I did, and now, instead of calling me "Miss Mia," they call me *Dai Mu Yi* (which I am told is a very good thing).

### Speaking Face

You will also give and gain face by learning the Chinese words for hello (*ni hao*), goodbye (*zaijian*), please (*qing*), thank you (*xie-xie*), you are welcome (*bu keqi*) and I am pleased to meet you (*hen gao xing jian dao ni*). (See Appendix II.) You don't need to overdo it. People from every culture enjoy foreigners' halting efforts at communicating in their language. You will not lose face.

### A Final Note on Face

When you contribute to the outward respect or prestige of the other party, you give face. This includes allowing room for the other person to elude, evade or stonewall to protect face. Other ways of giving and saving face include:

**QUICK TIP:**

Always attempt to make the other person look good.

*"The Chinese constantly want to show themselves at their best. They want to show their best face because they want others to respect and recognize them. They care about what others think and go to great lengths to prove that they are better."*

~ Yu-Hong (Beryl) Zhou, P. Eng., Siemens VDO Automotive Inc.

- reciprocity and returning a favor (Secret #4)
- treating people in authority with deference and respecting rank by using polite forms of address (Secret #7)
- avoiding pressure situations and respecting the decision-making process (Secret #8)
- treating business with appropriate seriousness (Secret #10)
- anticipating and compensating for miscommunications due to cultural and linguistic differences (Secret #13)
- following correct protocols (Part II)

Just about every Secret in this book comprises the concept of face, which is central to all interactions in Asia. There's no escaping it. Never forget that in a high-context culture, where everything relates to everything, the potential to cause loss of face through breaks in protocol is huge. If you were to do nothing else to protect your company's investment in the East, it would have to be to take care of face and surface harmony. Do that, and most everything else will fall right into place.

# SECRET #7:
# Understand, Respect and Abide by the Pecking Order

> *"It still makes me uncomfortable to argue with my boss, even after a Western education in China and five years working in North America."*
>
> ~ Calvin Wang, Product Engineer, Siemens VDO Automotive Inc.

The ground staff of an American airline was attempting to upgrade a young businessman to business class on a flight to Japan. He kept politely refusing their generous offer. They assured him there was no extra charge. He would not be inconveniencing anyone. They would be very happy if he would accept their offer. The man became quite anxious and finally explained that he could not possibly accept the upgrade offer. The reason? His boss had a seat booked in business class.

How unusual this seems against a Western backdrop, where social and business relationships have become so casual. But it's the way things are done in Asia. The respect for authority explains why bright people are not willing to voice their opinions in meetings. It is also the reason Western-style brainstorming and beef sessions do not work with people of the Pacific Rim.

## The Big Divide

Asian social hierarchy rules all interactions. Deference must be shown to those in authority. In business meetings, one does not speak until the "boss" has spoken. One never interrupts. One does not dare to express an opposing opinion. There is a vertical divide that protects face for both "boss" and employee. People know the roles that they are expected to play. Managers want, expect, and demand a show of respect from subordinates, in very specific ways. And if you manage employees with an Asian background and education, you will enjoy their full productivity only when you take into account their deeply programmed need to show respect to authority.

Calvin Wang received a Western university education in China and worked there as an electrical engineer for ten years before moving to Canada. Calvin says that, even after five years in corporate North America, he is still uncomfortable speaking up to his manager to express a different opinion. He still carries the cultural imprint of his schooling, where he was taught to show respect to anyone in authority. As Calvin explains, "To show respect, we cannot show that we are smarter or quicker than the boss. You always wait for him to express his opinions first. People of Asian culture are taught that it is not good to be too smart because that does not show respect to the boss. It disturbs the order, and you could be punished."

## The Talented Mr. Yang

Calvin's fear of insubordination no doubt goes back to early childhood, when cultural values are transmitted through stories and school day rituals. One of the most popular stories involves Cao Cao, a poet king of the Han Dynasty:

King Cao Cao loved riddles. He would often challenge his ministers to guess their meaning. His first secretary, Yang Xiu, was a talented scholar who regularly succeeded at deciphering the king's cryptic messages.

Yang Xiu did not stop with the word games. One day, quite by accident, he came across the king's military strategy. He immediately set about decoding it. Now knowing what the king's strategy would require of him, he ordered his troops to decamp. He anticipated great honor, and perhaps reward, when the king learned of his cleverness. But when word got back to the court, Cao Cao was outraged. He ordered Yang Xiu executed on the spot. Poor Yang Xiu's head was mounted on a gatepost as a warning to others who would dare to usurp the king's authority.

The moral of the story, in Calvin's words: "Your wisdom is related to your rank or class. You shouldn't show that you are smarter than the person in authority. So when a group of people is sitting together, even if the smartest person in the group interrupts his boss, others will be very uncomfortable with him."

## The Workings of Rank and Status

### *First, Employment*

A person's rank, status and prestige depend upon place of employment. Everyone who works for a highly ranked company shares in its perceived prestige in the marketplace. This holds true from the grassroots to the CEO level. That recognition is the purpose of the lapel pin. Loyalty is to the company first, not to the profession. If you ask what a person does for a living, the response will be, I am a member of the staff of Haier Group or Toyota or Samsung. Not, I am an engineer or purchaser or salesperson. There is almost no communication with members of one's profession outside the work circle and professional associations do not exist.

**Japan**

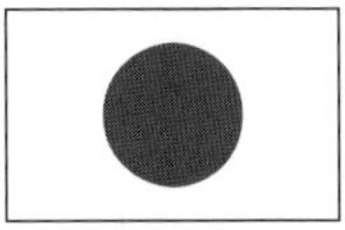

**QUICK TIP:**

Avoid causing loss of face through any comment or compliment on youthful appearance; this applies to both men and women.

### *Second, Schooling*

Education is the second factor in determining rank and status. Interestingly, prestige comes not from one's profession but from one's alma mater. The higher the school's standing, the higher the status of the individual. This is why there is such intense competition for acceptance into top-ranked universities. The prestige extends to one's entire family.

### *Third, Seniority*

The third indication of rank is seniority. Within the corporate power structure, groups are ranked by seniority, according to year of hiring. Since age is revered, even to suggest that a person may be too young to remember a certain event (considered a compliment in Western culture) may cause the Asian to lose face. You are implying that the person is too young to warrant your respect.

### *Then, Harmony*

Next is the ability to get along well with others. Promotions go to the person who maintains harmony, and can be counted on to care about the welfare of all.

### *Ability?*

Ability comes last.

**China**

*"It's considered better to work for a large company with a good reputation because people will respect you."*
~Yu-Hong (Beryl) Zhou, Polymer Specialist, Siemens VDO Automotive Inc.

## Chinese Status

Business reflects the hierarchy of rank and status to a lesser extent than in Japan and South Korea due to Communist influence. However, Chinese are very status conscious. They are impressed by degrees from Ivy League schools. They consider it important to show status through outward displays of wealth. You will experience this first hand if they invite you to dinner at a restaurant—at the cost of a month's salary.

Name brand imported items are popular, including designer clothing and accessories. People may not yet have money for homes or cars, but they are very well dressed. (And most still do not understand why we would lower our own status by wearing jeans and cut-offs. For this reason, save the sweat suits for exercise and alone time.)

*Guanxiwang*—the power to get things done through one's connections—is another visible sign of status. The better-connected one is, the more value one accumulates for future exchange purposes, the greater one's status and prestige. (You can read more on that topic in Secret #4: Think in Terms of a Web of Relationships.)

### "Whispering Humbleness"

> *"The superior man is modest in his speech, but exceeds in his actions."*
> ~ Confucius, Chinese philosopher (c. 551– 479 B.C.)

The show of humility as a virtue is deeply rooted in the Asian character. Humility, like face, affects all aspects of the business relationship, from the first greeting, to the business card exchange with bows and formal introductions, to how compliments are received. From childhood, they are taught to be modest. The lesson is, "No matter how great you are, you always can learn."

Appearance is deceiving. The show of humility cuts across rank and status. Even powerful, intelligent, wise people go to great lengths not to show their mental gifts. Often, the more powerful the person, the greater the show of humility.

But it would be an insult to treat the person the way he is acting. This means that you must proceed cautiously in establishing a new relationship. It will take time to determine who is the highest-ranking person. You will need to observe the subtle cues of rank and status before meeting with the players.

> **QUICK TIP:**
> Show of humility does not indicate status.

### After You, Mr. Wu

Protocol requires that Asians enter the room in order of seniority (determined by age and rank). This applies to business meetings and after-hour social occasions, not just in the more formal context of negotiations. The practice provides important clues for you: it tells you who expects to be shown the greatest respect. This is important to know, since varying levels of politeness are required, depending on the person's rank and status.

Likewise, Asians will assume that the first person in your group or delegation to enter the room is the senior person. That is the person to whom they will show the greatest deference. And that is the person whom they expect will lead the discussion from your side.

**QUICK TIP:**

In meetings with Asian customers, do not speak until the senior person has directed you to do so.

### Don't Be Gauche

In meetings, the most important person sits in the center, facing the door. The hierarchy extends to restaurant seating. If you are the guest of honor, you will sit in the middle of the table, facing the door. The next highest-ranking person will be on your right. Your Asian host will sit opposite you. The next highest-ranking person will be at his or her right. And the pattern repeats itself. The proper protocol is to wait for your host to point out where you will sit.

To not follow the above procedures is confusing to Asians. Conversely, following established rules of etiquette when you are hosting Asian guests will prove reassuring to them. Your meetings and other business interactions will go much more smoothly.

### Third Person Respect

Using the third person form of address (rather than the word "you") is a sign of great respect. Note that use of the title before the name adds more face.

- "Does Mr. Director wish to comment on our proposal?"
- "Would Mrs. Wu please sit at my right at dinner tonight?"
- "Would Mr. Wong do me the honor of visiting our offices the next time he is in the West?"

### Put Status on the Agenda

Find out ahead of time the rank and status of everyone who will be attending the meeting. If you are not able to ascertain the pecking order in advance of the meeting, show the greatest respect to the oldest Asian in the group, since age confers rank (although it is not the sole determinant). Take a moment after the exchange of business cards to study the card. Your Asian customer's business card will show the person's rank and status. You are expected to act accordingly.

Show your own rank and status as well. Make sure your business card reflects your company's prestige, your education, and your authority. In your conversation, position your company's size, technology, and global reach.

During initial greetings, stand to the right of the person who is introducing you. (Since the rank and status of the person who introduces you extends to you, this should also be thought out ahead of time.)

Acknowledge and shake hands with the most senior person first. Do not sit down until you have been invited to do so.

And remember to never interrupt.

### The Rank and Status of the Female Sex

In China, women are accepted as equals in higher levels of business. During the Cultural Revolution, women were expected to work, both in the government and private sectors. They have equal education opportunities and work is considered their contribution to family and society. Performing well reflects on their family.

**China**

Respect shown to seniority and rank applies equally to women in the boardroom. Women do not receive preferential treatment from their male colleagues. Men do not help them with their coats, open doors, or let them enter the room first.

So, there is no apparent sexism in Chinese business. However, those in the know say there are still economic and social inequalities.

Unlike Western women, Chinese women do not want to look young, because youth deprives them of status. For that reason, you are advised not to make observations about their youthful appearance. Comments that you may consider complimentary may cause embarrassment and loss of face.

**Japan**

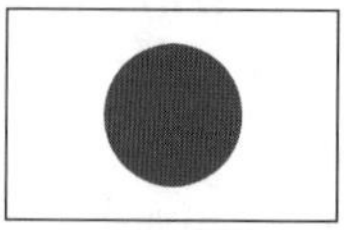

**South Korea**

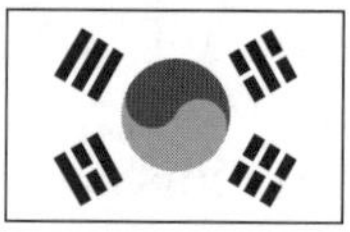

**QUICK TIP (FOR WOMEN):**

If offered a drink, you should accept, take a sip and set it aside.

### If You are a Woman, It's No Cakewalk

Male dominance is strong in Japan and South Korea. Barriers exist and women must work around them to succeed. If you are a woman, the best way for you to prevail is to be patient and to curb the impulse to come on strong. Allow time for the Asian businessman to appreciate your expertise, humility, knowledge, ability, and dependability. Working for a top-ranked firm, possessing impeccable credentials, and having the hide of a rhinoceros will ease the process. A great sense of humor (which you keep to yourself) will keep you sane.

You must not take offense at the male business rituals, praised in men and scorned in women. Women should not smoke. Women should not drink alcoholic beverages, and certainly, never to excess. Women should not laugh. Yes, this is a sexist double standard—and it's a reality.

But think of it this way: time and again, women have shown they are often better equipped to deal with the complexities and nuances of communication in high-context cultures. Be glad of this great asset.

# SECRET #8:
# Pray to the Right Buddha

Power, power, who has the power? That depends. In China, the decision-making process hinges on the magnitude of the decision.

## Big Decisions

In major decisions, the process is top-down and the one who has the power is fondly known as the Buddha. At a government level, power resides with a senior bureaucrat who is responsible for overseeing foreign investment and business ventures. On the company level, the real "boss" (CEO, GM or President) has absolute power for everything. In many companies, he is "the King." Nobody can easily change his decision without causing loss of face. In smaller enterprises, it is the patriarch or matriarch.

You can't just go by titles, however. As a Chinese friend told me, "Somebody may have a big title in the company [like VP or Chairman of the Board] and yet be nobody in the process of decision-making. It is just a title to keep them happy and quiet."

So, in companies, the Buddha is largely unknown. And that is your challenge. The actual power of department managers often depends on their relationship with the *real* "boss."

**China**

*"'Pray to the right Buddha' means you need to talk to the one who has real power in this matter. If you go to the wrong people, the right Buddha may block your case just because he has lost his face."*

~ Calvin Wang, Product Engineer, Siemens VDO Automotive Inc.

**QUICK TIP (CHINA):**

Find the right Buddha.

## Little Decisions: Think Collaboration, Build Group Consensus

A slow, structured, and layered decision-making process

applies to most everyday business dealings (as it does in Japan; see below). However, Calvin Wang, a Chinese born and educated engineer, gives another perspective: "If for some reason the boss shows great interest to go in a certain direction, everything goes very fast. So if you want everybody in the company to agree with and sign off your case, the best way is to let them know the boss is eager to see a positive answer. People are always easy to those who have a 'link to the sky.'"

### Link to the Sky

Once again, we see the critical importance of the web of personal relationships in connecting you to the right person who will lobby on your behalf. On your own, you could be dealing with many false Buddhas. Pray that your web of relationships includes someone whose *guanxiwang* includes people with mutual obligations to those who will influence the decision (Secret #4). Better still, pray, then hire a liaison with the right connections (Secret #5).

### Who is Responsible? No One. Everyone.

**Japan**

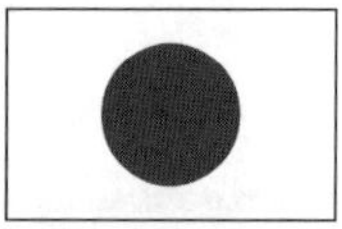

*"You ask, who is responsible? The answer is everybody. We agreed. We came to consensus. No single person can be dominantly responsible."*
~ Nate Iikubo, Advance Purchasing, Japanese automotive Tier 1 firm (Detroit, Michigan, USA)

Japanese do not like to be asked, "Who is responsible?" or "Who makes the decision?" They simply do not know how to respond. These are double-bind questions that cannot be answered without loss of face. They do not want to sound irresponsible. Yet there is no way to respond in a way that satisfies the Westerner because Japanese decision-making is collective and by consensus.

It is often impossible to pinpoint a main contact. There is no one single person you can go to.

Management is participative rather than authoritarian. The manager's role is to maintain harmony and a spirit of community, not to direct. To look after subordinates as they look out for him. Everyone in the group shares responsibility equally for successes and failures. That being the case, we have to consider every relationship strategic.

**QUICK TIP (JAPAN):**

Forget individual initiative. Seek the endorsement of the group.

It is important to develop rapport at various levels of the company with anyone who in any way touches your account. Do not rely only on relationships with people that you consider key players. There are no key players. They are all key players.

### Think Slow, Structured, and Layered

It takes everyone's yes for the decision to pass, and only one person's no for it to fizzle. Decisions start at the grassroots level. Typically, information is gathered, reviewed and digested by people at the bottom of the pyramid. These are the contact people who make the initial evaluation. From there, approval is required from several layers: the assistant manager; the manager; the general manager of the department; possibly the general manager from other departments, such as Quality Engineering; then the Vice-President; and, depending on the financial value of the decision, the President may also become involved. So the weight of the decision is well distributed.

To speed the decision process, make sure that all parties receive the same information. Keep everyone in the loop.

This process applies to proposals, drawings, approval requests, and tooling purchase orders. Along the way, the item gets redrafted. That explains why the document looks so different as time goes by. And it works. This system builds cooperation and ensures the support of the majority of managers and their teams when new policies or programs are initiated. At the end of the process, people at all levels support the decision, because they have a stake.

*"The senior person just needs to sign off."*

~ NATE IIKUBO, ADVANCE PURCHASING, JAPANESE AUTOMOTIVE TIER 1 FIRM (DETROIT, MICHIGAN, USA)

### Majority Rules

> "Consensus building is important and enforced. So you can't act alone. You can only act with consensus. The majority of people in upper positions have a good appreciation for the various levels of approval. The weight of the decision-making is not as great for the decision-maker because they are surrounded by people who were part of the process and support the decision. They are supported by and able to depend on those above and below them. No one person can be singled out. Everyone acts for the good of the company and fellow employees. So the senior person just needs to sign off."
>
> ~ NATE IIKUBO, ADVANCE PURCHASING, JAPANESE AUTOMOTIVE TIER 1 FIRM (DETROIT, MICHIGAN, USA)

**South Korea**

**QUICK TIP (SOUTH KOREA):**

To get to a decision-maker, do as you would in the West.

### More Westernized Decisions

In stark contrast, the final decision is always made by the manager in Korea, where business developed under the influence of the West. There is always a strong team focus and input is sought from others, but the final decision is often left to the one individual. And because of great respect for authority, that person's word is law. As in the West, when the system is working well, the best decision-makers get promoted to positions of increasing authority. So your best strategy to get things done in Korea is to talk to the person who has the big picture.

Koreans realized some time ago that layers had to be eliminated if decisions were to be made more quickly. Since the mid-1990's, many Korean companies have eliminated layers in the organization and structured themselves more like North American firms. Although the change to a flatter structure was difficult, it was considered necessary to facilitate decision-making and improve productivity.

**MILLION DOLLAR MISTAKE #8:**

Pushing for an answer before they are ready to give it. Because they will just shut you out.

### Do Not Create Passive Resistance

The Western system rewards good, independent decision-making. We value the philosophy of individual accountability. And that does not prepare us for the reaction we get in the East. When you pressure your Asian customers for a decision, you are asking them to defy their instincts, their culture, and their training. More than likely, you will create a scenario of passive resistance.

They will go quiet, submissive, and outwardly non-resistant, because you have placed them in an impossible position. No one will refuse you directly, because that would be rude. Yet they will not act, because they cannot act alone. So the decision you want will stall. You will be left hanging.

### Strategy for the Consensus Process

The consensus process takes so long that you need a strategy to help move the process along. First, respect the process. Allow sufficient time for what you know will be a lengthier process than you are accustomed to.

1. Work with a cooperative spirit. When you are on-site, talk and be friendly with everyone you meet.
2. One person in your group or delegation will speak for your entire group. During negotiations and even social occasions, that person will sit to the right of the spokesperson for the Asian group. That is the seat of honor.
3. Develop parallel team structures and roles for collaboration. For example, allowing more than one person to speak on your behalf confuses the consensus process. It violates Asian protocol and slows things down.

Appendix VI: The Working Papers Way to Trust, presents a blueprint for achieving consensus step-by-step with those who interact with Buddha.

4. Make sure every member of your team has been briefed on the proper protocols. Interruptions and disagreements between group members put you in very bad light.
5. Make sure that all parties receive the same information. Provide a package of information needed to make the decision (past history, past agreements—if applicable, data, figures, charts and statistics). In addition, keep all your contacts in the communication loop by copying them on all written and email follow-up correspondence.
6. Plan to present your case in one organized stroke. (If you come back later with bits of information, you will further slow down the decision-making process, because they may feel the need to go back to the beginning.)
7. Factor in that they may come back to you with a request for more information. Have your backup information at your fingertips, in case they want more data.
8. Expect that many meetings will be scheduled to discuss and get consensus on even small points.

# SECRET #9:
# In Asia, Business is Personal and Emotional

Asians want a personal connection before doing business. All relationships are personal relationships. Business and social life merge. Many social needs are met on the job. Anything you can do to help meet these needs and strengthen the personal side of the relationship will repay you many times over. Decisions will come more quickly when you nourish the personal side. As a client told me, "What's a $100 golf game to a $5M contract?"

### Family Ties

In Western cultures, business life is compartmentalized. It is separate from and often thought to be secondary to personal life and religious or political practice. It is acceptable to have a personal life away from the office. In Asian cultures, business life is considered more important than personal life, and one's commitment is expected to be total. One works longer hours in return for employer loyalty. Identification with work is closer than with family, and colleagues are considered family.

**MILLION DOLLAR MISTAKE #9:**

Not socializing with your Asian colleagues after hours.

In any culture, of course, people will say family is their top priority. But the way people from different cultures go about demonstrating that conviction varies significantly. A Japanese living in America explained the difference this way:

> "In North America, you would be seen as addicted, intrigued, and obsessed by your work if you worked 15 hours a day. You would be seen as not living up to family obligations. Your spouse would say, find a job that demands less of your time. The Asian mindset is far different.

> In order to support my family, since I am part of the company, I am the company and the company is me. And that's the collective good. It's the formula. It's the unwritten rule of engagement. I have to do it for the collective good. Of course, I love my family, and here, perhaps, is how I best show it. I make sacrifices for the company and they take care of me. So in return, I place unquestioning priority on the company. My family understands."

### Business After Hours

The Asian desire for personal connection requires much more personal investment than you may be accustomed to. Even in the initial negotiation process, forging a lasting relationship is more important than hammering out a good agreement. Eating, drinking, karaoke, and spending time together after hours all play a key role in business.

**QUICK TIP:**

When you are the guest, always leave the restaurant before they do.

After the meeting, the supplier usually invites the customer to dinner. Although business is not discussed after hours, the bonding that occurs is essential to your success. It would be a serious mistake—not to mention a serious breach of etiquette—to refuse the invitation. The same applies if you are visiting a plant and are invited to a meal as a guest. You are expected to eat in the cafeteria. Suggesting that you eat off-site is another breach of etiquette.

If you refuse an invitation to socialize, it gives the impression you do not want to mingle. Worse, you miss out on building the bond of trust, which is the keystone to your success.

### You Need to Get Drunk!

You have to at least appear to get drunk. It is the fastest way to break through to the inner circle. Drinking plays a crucial role in bridging the cultural gap. There are more chances of getting to know someone when defenses are down.

Asians say that you do not really know a man until you have been with him drunk, because drinking reveals a person's true character. The thick outer barrier of distrust and reserve dissolves. You get to see the real person. In any culture, what a person does when drunk is what they would do under a different type of pressure when sober.

Ultimately, of course, what counts is your ability to come through, to persevere through thick and thin, to get the job done. But drinking together makes life a lot easier.

> *"Koreans believe drinking is one of the key factors to become friends. But North Americans enjoy only a little bit of drinking. So the Korean man is different."*
> ~ Song Jong-Ho, Director Purchasing, Doowon Group

*Drinking Quick Tips:*

✓ Come into their circle by drinking—or appearing to drink—to excess.

✓ Accept that this is how things are in the culture. Do not act like they should be toning it down. Do not make them look like fools, or feel judged.

✓ As a non-drinker, showing disapproval of the amount of drinking that goes on will hurt the relationship between your companies.

✓ If you do not drink for religious or health reasons, excuse yourself and say why you are unable to drink. Then look like you're having a grand old time. You will be maintaining surface harmony, which is common practice and perfectly acceptable.

> **QUICK TIP:**
> Make your Asian clients feel at home by including them in local activities.

**Business Entertaining on Home Turf**

When Asians are on your home turf, you must reciprocate with the same attentiveness that they would give you. It's simply not enough to treat them to one or two dinners and

**QUICK TIP:**

Maintain the relationship through entertaining customers every few months.

then drop your guests off at their hotel to fend for themselves. They would not dream of doing that to you. Without social interaction and companionship with groups of people, your Asian guests will feel alone and abandoned. It breaks the bond that you are striving to maintain.

Westerners need to show greater hospitality. This includes entertaining every evening and on weekends. Take them on tours of the surrounding region. Treat them to cultural and sporting events. Take them to the horse races. Show them the local color. My clients have included their Asian customers in activities such as cow tipping and raccoon hunting. They loved it. For months, it was the topic of conversation.

*Home Turf Quick Tips:*

✓ Find out what your customer likes to do. Then make it happen. Take it over the top. Plan for a little surprise on top of a planned event. For example, buy your guest a Titleist hat or golf balls after the golf game. The symbolic gesture is unexpected and welcome. Or throw in a spontaneous dinner invitation. Or an unexpected visit to a local landmark.

✓ Have your customer fly in on a Saturday night. Plan to do something social together on Sunday. You can include your family. Asians are curious about Westerners. They like to be invited to your home. They love to be involved in local events.

✓ Seek out restaurants that appeal to the Asian palate. When they are far from home, and in a totally different culture to their own, it makes sense that they would crave familiar foods. Remember the Chinese expression: "When the belly is happy, the man is happy."

# SECRET #10:
# Treat Asian Business as Serious, Very Serious

In the more relaxed business atmosphere of the West, good-natured teasing, bantering, and camaraderie are a sign of colleagues working well together. Humor, sometimes expressed as sarcasm, is an effective tool to ease the stress and defuse tense situations.

But that same laughter creates stress and tension in the East. Asians do not use humor to lighten things up at work. It causes insult and can result in loss of face. Business is no laughing matter.

> *"They were talking in English and they were laughing. That seemed unreasonable. We felt they were laughing at us. They had the best proposal. We did not give them the contract."*
>
> ~ Name withheld, Asian Executive

## THE BUSINESS MEETING IS SERIOUS

Make it absolutely clear to your Asian contacts that you value and respect their business and their time. To demonstrate this, schedule appointments in advance. Never drop in unannounced for sales calls. Be punctual for your appointments; being late is a serious insult. Go in prepared to dedicate the meeting to business. Do not make small talk. Do not replay last night's game with your Western colleagues. Do not discuss family matters. Save the humor for the evening's social event.

> **QUICK TIP:**
>
> When making presentations, avoid the North American penchant for opening with a joke or humorous anecdote. This will be interpreted as showing lack of respect for the subject matter, the audience, and the companies in attendance.

There is a difference between taking your client's business seriously and taking yourself too seriously. Be modest, respectful, polite, and a little bit humble. Never do anything that could be construed as arrogant or rude.

Needless to say, avoid humorous or sarcastic commentary.

And never forget the importance of surface harmony and face. Do not argue. Do not interrupt. Do not contradict the customer or your own manager in the meeting. You may disagree in private, but never in a group situation. The good news is that the pace of a typical meeting agenda in Asia is slower than in the West. This gives you time to think things through before you speak. Use it! Choose your words carefully and do not think out loud.

### The Perils of Brainstorming

> **QUICK TIP:**
>
> Never speak off the top of your head. Think it through first.

Brainstorming is the first sacred cow to be sacrificed in Asia. It may produce cultural clashes rather than valuable new ideas. Furthermore, many of the factors that make brainstorming successful will be missing from your meeting. Brainstorming requires that everyone around the table be fluent in the spoken language. Both language and communication style present barriers. Most Asians are more comfortable with the written word, which is more formal and precise than speaking off the cuff. In addition, Asians' interpersonal style favors frequent, long, serious face-to-face meetings. Brainstorming sessions run counter to these expectations.

> **QUICK TIP:**
>
> Forget the freewheeling brainstorming rules they taught you in management class.

Brainstorming encourages the use of humor and show of emotion to stimulate creativity. It encourages people to interrupt one another and speak without stopping to think or judge their thoughts. But these factors are the exact opposite of what's required when working in Asia. Face and surface harmony depend upon the ability to suppress and control one's emotions, even those that would seem positive.

Finally, brainstorming requires equality around the table. Everyone's ideas are treated equally and without hierarchy: they are all valuable and potentially laughable.

But in a status-conscious culture, where acknowledging rank is critical to maintaining face, this presents an impossible situation. In meetings, Asians observe a strict hierarchical code. According to business practice, they will generally meet to discuss business with senior officials of the same or parallel rank. (It is a serious breach of this protocol to send someone of an inferior rank to represent you.) Brainstorming simply breaks with too many protocols required for making headway with your Asian customers. It is best to avoid it.

*Meeting Protocol Quick Tips:*

- ✓ When entering the room, the highest-ranking member of your team should lead the way.
- ✓ In a meeting room, sit facing the door, not with your back to the door.
- ✓ Senior and higher ranked participants are always introduced first, followed by younger and lower ranked participants.
- ✓ The highest-ranking person speaks first, others when spoken to.
- ✓ When using an interpreter, speak directly to the person you are having a conversation with. Pause after every two or three sentences to avoid overloading the interpreter.
- ✓ When you are on their turf, leave the meeting room before they do.

## THE SUPPLIER RELATIONSHIP IS SERIOUS

### Mistakes are Serious

A large part of the seriousness revolves around the Asian's fear of making a mistake, of being wrong. If you make a mistake, you are not to be trusted.

If you have to advise your Asian customer about an error or problem, plan it through from every angle before making the call. What are you going to do to remedy it? Don't let your customer find out about the problem first. Be proactive and be the one to tell them. This will help redeem you.

*"When the customer requires support, you arrive very soon. We had a serious, urgent problem. The supplier called back from Toulouse, France and said, 'I am leaving on my holiday. I planned it several months ago.' It ruined the relationship."*

~ Xu Baoping, CEO, Siemens VDO Electric Motor (Shanghai) Co. Ltd.

### Problems are Serious

As a supplier, you are in the inferior position. When problems arise that your Asian customers consider critical and urgent, they expect you to drop everything you are doing and come to the rescue. Someone in your organization has to be readily available 24/7, even on holidays, to deal with inevitable crises. Fulfilling these obligations adds to the positive history of the relationship and provides opportunity for future reciprocity.

### Potential Problems are Serious

Finding the potential crisis, difficulty or shortage is important in Asian culture. Asians are taught to discuss potential problems, project potential risks into the future, and prepare for the worst-case scenario from the outset. As one of my Chinese colleagues says, "In our culture, we like to imagine the worst. We will mention the difficulty. It is our duty to be serious, to be responsible. It has a positive side, because once the program is launched, it is problem-free. But the initial part is very long."

This cautious approach conflicts with the positive, optimistic outlook of the West. Here, managers will push ahead with projects, provided the risk scenarios are reasonable. Although there is always potential for failure, there is a certain tolerance for issues that will invariably arise during implementation. For every problem (if it even comes up) a solution will be found.

A common misstep by foreign companies is to under-deliver during the planning phase. Calvin Wang, Product Engineer with Siemens, says it is a mistake to dismiss your Asian customers' concerns as pessimistic or nit-picking: "Japanese customers always find new or potential problems that may turn out to be not an issue. But if, as a supplier, we say that's not important at all and it's not an issue based on our experience, without providing enough solid evidence, they will be unhappy or even angry. They want as much evidence as possible to prove it is not a problem. They want all the details. Finding potential problems is very good."

## The "Japanese Way"

**Japan**

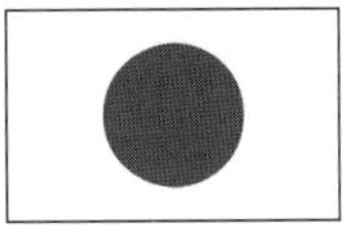

In Japan, the rules of business are based on old religious practices. Workers undergo an intense conditioning in the "Japanese Way"—manners, rules of conduct, obligations, like-thinking, and "instinctive unselfishness."

There is a strong work ethic and they strive for perfection in all that they do. The Japanese and South Koreans work very long hours for the collective good, or out of deference to their managers. What other culture in the world has a word to describe death by overwork (*karoshi*)?

Japan's largest labor union group, the Japanese Trade Union Confederation (Rengo) compiled data from 23,000 unionized workers who responded to a survey on overtime work in late 2002. They reported, "Over 50% of unionized workers in Japan work overtime without pay an average of 29.6 hours per month." Those who do not work overtime "do not show the right attitude towards the company."[3]

In 2003, the union at Honda Motor Company put its foot down and said that their engineers could no longer work past 10:00 p.m.!

**Korea**

### To Work Hard is to Work Long

"I have to show my boss I am working very hard—even on weekends. They value that, even if the results aren't there. [Westerners] work very intensely from 8 until 5. Koreans work 12 hours, but intensely for four hours only. We chat, drink coffee, socialize. We pretend we work 12 hours. Bosses over 50 believe we work hard if we work long."

~ Song Jong-Ho, Director Purchasing, Doowon Group (Seoul, Korea)

# SECRET #11:
# The Meaning is in What They Don't Say

In the West, we love debate, logic, facts, open discussion, rationality, and taking a strong position. In all these instances, good verbal skills are a benefit. Managers like clarity, and there is not a lot of tolerance for ambiguity or "beating around the bush."

In Asian cultures, communication is never that simple. The culture of surface harmony requires silence, noncommitment, and avoidance of friction at all costs. Communication is indirect and often unspoken. Asians will not explain exactly what they want you to do or how they want you to do it. The tone of voice is more important than the words used. Nuance and silence carry great meaning, and that meaning is easily missed by the untrained eye and ear.

**QUICK TIP:**

Ask yourself, "What is not being said here? Could it be more important than what I'm hearing?"

## Silence is Golden

In any culture, it is almost always better to say too little than too much. This is especially true in Asian cultures. The Koreans say, "Speech is silver, silence is golden." The Japanese say, "Hollow drums make the most noise." Simply translated, they all say we Westerners talk too much.

*"A wise man hears one and understands ten."*
~ Old Chinese proverb

Most of us find silence uncomfortable. We have an impulse to fill the void whenever there is a gap in the conversation. But for Asians, silence is considered useful. It is a time to think and process information and explore what is being said. It is a way to communicate respect. It is also a way to disagree with what is being said without confrontation.

**QUICK TIP:**

Laughter, humor, sarcasm and jest are out of context in business meetings and on the plant floor.

### Laughter Does Not Mean Ha-Ha

Laughter is not limited to expressions of joy and mirth in Asian cultures. As a Korean friend told me, seeing an Asian laugh or smile is like when you see a dog's teeth—you have to take its meaning from the context. It can express great pleasure. Then again, it may be an emotional valve for feelings of disappointment, embarrassment, sadness, confusion, shock, anger, or lack of understanding. When you witness a smile, therefore, consider the range of possibilities. Is there a chance that there's been a miscommunication? Have you made a request that is impossible to meet? Could you have given offense? Do you need to take rapid measures to restore face and surface harmony?

In Eastern cultures, real laughter comes from deep within. There is a saying, "Beware the man who, when he laughs, the belly doesn't move." As a Westerner, you will not often see the Asian belly move. Laughter is seldom raucous. Take your cues from your hosts and do not laugh too loud, even after hours in a karaoke bar. Finally, if you are a woman, try not to laugh at all. It is part of a double standard that women are not expected to laugh unless they are part of the "entertainment industry."

# SECRET #12: Never Say "No"

"No" is a simple word that Westerners value. It is straightforward. From the Westerner's perspective, it shows honesty, transparency, and respect for the other person's time. But in the Asian context, "no" is considered rude and confrontational. Even shaking the head to mean "no" signals disrespect. It hurts the relationship. And it can lead to loss of face.

Unless we learn to recognize the many alternative signals for "no," we will give and receive the wrong message. For example, if an Asian says, "It is certainly worth thinking about," that really means, "Don't hold your breath." Similarly, "I'll think about it" often means, "It ain't gonna happen any time soon." This cuts both ways, of course. So if you respond to a request with, "We'll try to meet your needs on time," chances are you'll be interpreted as responding in the negative.

### Impossible Requests

Never refuse a request directly. Yun Kim is a Product Engineer with Siemens VDO Automotive Inc. In his supplier role, he knows the value of sidestepping direct confrontation that could damage the customer relationship. As he explains, "Asian customers will always request design changes. No is a rude and arrogant answer. Find another route. If [my Asian customer] gives me unrealistic timing, I don't say no. I never say no to [him]. I go to him and ask, 'What do you want me to do? What's our negotiation point?' I say: 'I will try to meet your need on time.' I always say I will try. My feeling, after three years, is that they like that attitude."

**QUICK TIP:**

Be indirect. Never refuse anything directly. Rather, give an explanation for why something is not possible.

### And if You Must Say No. . .

To protect relationships, you must absolutely avoid embarrassing people and causing loss of face in the presence of others. If possible, speak to the person in private, or even better, use an interpreter to convey your message indirectly.

Precede your words by sucking in a deep breath through your teeth. Make use of what you've learned about the art of the apology in Secret #6. Avoid giving an answer immediately, but if you must, then find a quiet, respectful way to say "no."

Practice using some indirect alternatives to "no":

- That will be a little difficult.
- It might be a problem.
- We will do our best.
- I need to talk to my director.
- We will consider it and give you our answer later.
- We will consider it. Leave it with us.
- We are in the process of studying the matter.

**QUICK TIP:**

When answering a question, give an explanation first, then respond indirectly.

### Put "No" on Paper

Finally, follow up your meeting with a clear, honest communication in writing, explaining why the request is not possible. Present all the data that support your conclusions. Stating your reasons is important for promoting trust between your two companies. You need to make it clear that although it is your greatest desire and honor to help your customers, circumstances make it impossible for you to meet their request at this time.

# SECRET #13:
# Take Responsibility for Poor Communication

The best definition of communication I have ever come across is this: *Communication is what the other person understood.* Not what you meant, but what the other person understood. If the other person did not get your meaning, then you have miscommunicated. Period.

Improve the communication, improve the relationship.

Sometimes, in cross-cultural training sessions, I get asked, "Why should we take all the responsibility for communication? Doesn't it go both ways?" I respond, "Because when we fail to do so we cause confusion, indecision, and costly production delays. We compromise trust and hurt the relationship. We have so much to lose. And we're really only ever in control of ourselves."

Brent Moorcroft is General Manager of the Power Train Management Business Unit for Johnson Electric's Hong Kong operations. He says, "I have customers calling me with very minor issues that my staff in North America used to deal with at their level, so that I would never hear about them: technical issues, quality issues, delivery issues, pricing issues. All because of poor communication."

*"Most Westerners think that most Asians speak English well. That is a big misunderstanding. The person who works in overseas marketing does, but the engineers and quality control people don't. Westerners make their presentations, unaware they are not being understood 100%. Asians have a lot of ideas, but it's hard to explain over the language barrier."*

~ JinSeung Lee, Applications Engineer, Motor Division, Siemens VDO Automotive Inc.

## Spoken English Offends the Pride

It helps to understand that most of your Asian colleagues are not fluent in spoken English. Although they may have spent close to 1,000 hours in the classroom learning English, the emphasis was on grammar, the written word, and passing the college entrance exams. They've had few opportunities to practice speaking the living language. Until recently, even their teachers were not fluent English speakers. So don't be fooled by their understanding of words on paper. With the possible exception of those under 30, the command of the spoken word is minimal.

For the highly motivated and otherwise accomplished Asian, this is a source of embarrassment. It offends their pride. The potential for failure causes them to avoid speaking English and looking foolish.

My Korean friend, JinSeung Lee, advises Westerners to be ever vigilant to ensure that real understanding is achieved. He explains:

> "When the Westerner doesn't understand, he will say: 'I'm sorry. I don't understand. Could you explain it again?' Most [Asians] won't ask you to explain it again. They just stay quiet and expressionless. If you see a lack of expression, it means you have not been understood."

*"Local people are very capable, but because they prefer to use written English through emails, the spontaneity of the communication is lost. So a topic that we can discuss thoroughly in a 10-minute telephone call can drag out for three or four days by exchange of emails because of the 12-hour time difference. Customers are impatient and call to speak with me directly when this starts to happen."*

~ Brent D. Moorcroft, General Manager, Power Train Management Business Unit, Johnson Electric (Hong Kong)

Then again, the expressionless face is a sign of sophistication. How are you to know the difference? Watch for the subtle clues of puzzlement: the questioning look in the eye, the slight inclination of the head. Above all, be sympathetic to the additional distress that the language barrier creates and take steps to alleviate it.

**QUICK TIP:**

If you see that you were not understood, say, "I am sorry that I was not clear. Let me say it a better way."

*Quick Tips for Better Communication:*

✓ Use an interpreter from the start, even when it appears that your Asian counterparts speak and understand English. To avoid offending their pride, point the responsibility back to you. Say, "Please allow me to have an interpreter here to assist me in making sure that I understand your needs."

✓ Avoid all slang, idioms, puns, sports language, and expressions that cannot be translated, such as "at the end of the day," "bite the bullet," and "doing an end run."

✓ Let your customer take time to think before answering. Do not interrupt the thought process. Allow long pauses. Do not feel that you have to jump in and fill the void. In turn, consider a matter for a while before giving your answer. Remember that speaking without thinking first is suspect. It is important to choose your words carefully and not think out loud with Asians.

✓ Find ways to save face. Plan to promote understanding in advance of the meeting. For example, provide written copies of your presentations, including charts, graphs, and other visuals to support your communication.

✓ Meet face-to-face whenever possible. In the West, communication by telephone and email is standard, but face-to-face communication and physical contact are preferred in the East. Note also that leaving a message

**QUICK TIP:**

When you are making a presentation for simultaneous translation, cut 30-35% of your material when you have to stick to a timed agenda. For the speak/stop/repeat method, cut 50-60% of your material.

**QUICK TIP:**

Send an outline of your material and PowerPoint slides to the translator or interpreter ahead of time.

**QUICK TIP:**

After you have presented your report, ask, "Do you have any questions?"

with someone other than the person you are calling is not recommended, as colleagues may not wish to take responsibility for transmitting the message.

### Common Faux Pas

*Wrong Person*

It is human nature to direct our conversation to the person who has the best English-language skills. This is an error because the person who speaks the best English may not necessarily be the most important or highest ranking person in the room. You could undercut the person's authority and cause loss of face.

*Patronizing Attitude*

Some people have the tendency to raise their voice, speak extra slowly, repeat themselves, use broken English, or talk more than they need to when communicating with someone who has not mastered the English language. This will be seen as condescension and is to be avoided.

**QUICK TIP:**

Don't raise your voice in an attempt to be understood.

*Lost in Translation*

When speaking through an interpreter, it is important to speak to the individual you are communicating with and not the interpreter. It is also important to think through exactly what you want to say. Find ways of saying it simply and clearly in three or four different ways, from different points of view. Spell things out. Pause after one or two sentences to allow the interpreter to absorb and process your words.

**QUICK TIP:**

Direct your conversation to the person you are communicating with, and not the translator or interpreter.

*Structural Differences*

Language shapes our thinking. It shapes our perceptions. It affects how we process information. Through language we filter all of life's experiences and develop different worldviews. So it may not be possible for Westerners to ever learn exactly how Asians think. But we can get insights into how they organize their thinking and process information through looking at the structure of the language.

For example, Asian sentence structure and word order differ from English. "I go to work" translates to "I work go." "They didn't meet with us" translates to "They not with us meet." Because they have to unscramble the word sequence to make sense of things, it's important to use simple sentences and speak at a slower pace. Another way to communicate better and avoid confusion is to use flag words to signal your meaning. Before asking a question, say: "I have a question."

**China**

Most Chinese languages have no verb tenses. This creates potential for misunderstanding about time frames. Therefore, do not simply rely on the use of verb tenses. Start and end your responses to questions with words that identify a specific point of time: "now," "later today," "tomorrow," "one week from now."

**Japan**

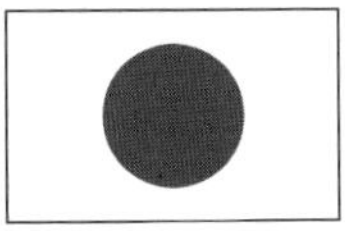

The Japanese language includes "markers" which are placed at the end of the sentence, and which alter the meaning of the sentence. The marker "*so*" means, "I'm in agreement with you." "*Ka*," accompanied by an upward inflection of the voice, indicates that a question is being asked.

I am told that the Japanese language has about one-tenth the consonant and vowel sounds of the English language, so this decreases their comprehension by about 90%.

## Formal vs. Informal

It helps to understand from the outset that Asian languages are much more formal, polite, and indirect than the English language. Watch your tone and avoid casual terms, such as "you guys." This level of familiarity is considered disrespectful. And do not interrupt. We have a high tolerance in the West for this inconsiderate habit. But in Asia it is strictly bad manners.

*7 Quick Communication Tips:*

1. Spend very little time talking. Listen and take notes. Even more important than listening for the words is listening for hesitation, which provides clues as to meaning. If you can capture the subtleties, it will pay you back later.
2. Make your needs and requirements (and the reasons behind them) known—clearly, quietly, consistently, and insistently.
3. Watch that your volume, tone, and quality of voice are not offensive. You can do that by matching and mirroring your Asian colleague's manner.
4. Use short, simple sentences and uncomplicated language. Speak slowly and clearly, pausing often to allow your words to be processed and understood. Pause before responding.
5. Answer questions specifically and one at a time.
6. Ask for clarification and ask a lot of questions. Before asking a question say, "I have a question." This will avoid confusion and misunderstanding.
7. Ask if they have any questions about what you are discussing. If you have been talking and there are no questions, it means you have not been understood. This gets complicated because of the need to give face. Even if you are quite sure that your Asian counterpart has not understood you, you may have to pretend she or he has, in order to maintain the relationship.

# SECRET #14:
# Keep Them from Saying "Yes" when They Mean "No"

A typical exchange, full of miscommunication and misperceptions despite honest intent, might go something like this:

*Westerner:* "You are not going to change the specifications at this late date, are you?"

*Asian:* "Yes." (Meaning, "Yes. We are not going to change the specifications at this late date.")

*Westerner:* "But that isn't what we agreed upon!"

The Westerner goes away muttering to himself: "You just can't count on these people. They say one thing and mean another." Meanwhile, the Asian thinks: "Foreigners! You just can't please them." The results are time delays and lost productivity.

*"The biggest problem we have in Asia is communication."*
~ Roland Bauer, Vice President and General Manager, Siemens VDO Automotive Inc.

**QUICK TIP:**
Use only positive sentences.

## The Many Faces of Yes

"Yes" does not always mean yes. Sometimes it means maybe. Sometimes "yes" may only be a sign of respect, a signal that you have been heard. Sometimes "yes" may even mean "no." There is no intended deception. Yes is simply a more complicated word in Asian culture.

In order to help you save face, Asians will not tell you that you are wrong. Even in a corporate setting, they will not tell you why your thinking is wrong. Nor will they risk offending you by saying "no." Rather, they will change the subject, or say nothing, or answer a question with a question. More than likely, your Asian customers mean "no" when they say something noncommittal that can be interpreted in any number of positive ways. "Let us study it" or "Let's discuss this another time" may mean "Forget it!" "This is an unusual request" translates to "Don't hold your breath."

### No "Yes-No" Questions

Since "yes" is often only an acknowledgement, you want to avoid questions that invite a "yes" or "no" response. Ask questions that require specific information in response. Rather than saying, "I need that information as soon as possible," Say, "When can we expect that information?" Or, "What time may I expect that information in the morning?" Or, "What do you need from me in order to have that information for tomorrow's meeting?" The nature of the answer will indicate whether or not you have communicated well and been fully understood.

### Is That a Yes or a No?

Use only positive sentences. If you use negatively phrased questions, you will get a blank stare or an unintended response. This applies to tag questions, such as, "You didn't mean that, did you?" Rather than replying with a "no" as we do, the Asian will reply with a "yes," meaning, "Yes, I didn't mean that."

Avoid double negatives, because they are confusing in any context and especially for Asians. They have no first-language equivalent to translate statements like, "It happens not infrequently" or "I'm not saying there isn't a solution to this problem."

When you think everyone understands, verify comprehension by asking an open-ended question that requires an informed response. For example, "What is your solution to the problem?"

## Do It in Writing

Most Asians' comprehension of written English is far better than their verbal skills. After every meeting, put it in writing—clearly, simply, and grammatically, without slang or idioms. When you are in agreement, write, "I agree."

Do not count on one memo to communicate. People get busy. They set messages aside. You may need to follow up from different angles to make your point.

# SECRET #15:
# Three Qualities Will Help You Succeed in Asia: Interpersonal Flexibility, the Ability to Detach, and the Ability to Tolerate Ambiguity

Too often, companies select a top performer to represent them in Asia, without considering the personal qualities that make for success in the East. Our top performers (particularly top sales performers) are often assertive, independent, fast-paced, no-nonsense, straight-shooting, get-me-to-the-decision-maker types. They have the strong handshake and direct eye contact and ability to get things done that we so value. Yet all of these qualities have to be suppressed because they are counterproductive when working with Asian customers, suppliers and local staff. Other qualities have to be developed in order to succeed.

## INTERPERSONAL FLEXIBILITY

To bridge the gap between the cultures and connect with people whose ways differ from our own, we need to be willing to adapt our personal style.

### How Will You Adapt Your Style to the Following Three Facts?

1. *Asians are more reserved and harder to get to know.* It can take years. Even then, to what extent can you really be trusted as a foreigner? Asians perceive Westerners as aggressive, impatient and impulsive. This can be used against you if you are not aware of, and able to adapt your outward behaviors: how fast you walk; how loud and fast you talk; your display of emotions.

**QUICK TIP:**

Do not even sigh in frustration.

2. *Asians' use of time is less structured.* In the West, we think of time as linear. In the East, time is circular and relative and connected to past history. So Asians don't have the same sense of urgency. Better to make the right decision than rush things along. Attempting to force your sense of urgency on your Asian clients will only result in passive resistance.
3. *Asians care deeply about how others see them.* Their interpersonal behavior exists to protect and give face while maintaining surface harmony. Their ways of behaving bear no relationship to how they really feel about the other person.

### Act Unnatural

In Western culture, the face and body contribute a lot of information to a conversation. You can communicate instantly simply by smiling, frowning, laughing out loud, even pounding your fist on the table. But that will hurt you in the Asian business context. You need to become less transparent, not so easy to read.

*Monitor your assertiveness.* Keep your emotions in check. Suppress the facial animation. Check your hand and body gestures. Stay composed and rein in the enthusiasm. Relax the handshake, tone down the eye contact and stand back. Speak slowly and quietly. Move slowly and deliberately.

*Change how you deliver information.* Slow down. Ask questions instead of making statements. Never come right to the point. Start with background information, describe each point of decision, then end with your recommendation. (Do not start with your conclusion and work backward. That will work against you.)

**QUICK TIP:**

Slow down. Take a quiet, deep breath. Wipe that expression off your face.

*"In working with Honda, you have to tell a story. Everything you do has to have a beginning, a middle and an end. The Japanese always look at things from the beginning. So start from the condition, then your analysis, then the conclusion—even when it's something that's blatantly obvious."*

~ Name withheld, Automotive Client

*Remove any hint of challenge or confrontation.* Never interrupt. Refrain from displaying or forcing your ideas on others. Keep your (strong) opinions to yourself.

*Protect personal dignity.* Seek to maintain surface harmony by smoothing over misunderstandings. Accept responsibility for communication breakdowns.

*Drop the sense of urgency.* Pause before responding. Under-react rather than overreact. Never show exasperation. Do not even sigh in frustration. Finally, during business hours, skip the small talk, personal stories and humor altogether.

This all requires most Westerners to act in ways that feel unnatural. For some of us, it's exhausting to keep ourselves on such a tight leash. At the end of this chapter, I will suggest ways to compensate and release the tension before it gets to you.

## THE ABILITY TO DETACH

Detachment is the ability to step back and disengage from events, to see ourselves objectively. It prevents us from applying pressure and turning off the other party.

In any communication, the person who has the ability to walk away holds the stronger position. Conversely, the inability to detach personally makes us susceptible to manipulation.

Detachment serves many useful purposes when you cannot be in control of the factors that result in delays and prolonged decision-making. Because detachment encounters no resistance, it minimizes delays. It enables you to put a distance between yourself and whatever has the potential to cause anxiety and stress. It allows you to process information without interference from your emotions. It keeps you from foot-in-mouth disasters that result from speaking too soon.

*"Never show frustration. When I first started working with an Asian customer, I showed impatience at the 15-month mark. That was a mistake. When I became more relaxed about it, saying, 'I may lose this,' I got the business."*

~ Joe Varghese, Customer Projects Manager, Motor Division, Siemens VDO Automotive Inc.

To stay detached in the moment, think and plan in advance how you are going to handle contingencies. Don't allow a sense of urgency to interfere with your ability to remain neutral. Chinese in particular are very strong negotiators. They will use your sense of urgency against you. They will postpone a decision on critical issues right to the deadline when they know you have a plane to catch.

Step back from your usual vantage point and take delight in the fascinating textures of a high-context culture where everything connects to everything, where truth is relative, and where issues of face affect every transaction. Appoint another person to take notes. Get comfortable with periods of silence and use that time to watch and learn. Make it your goal to observe the details of interactions. Watch how information flows from one person to another. Note the subtle cues of unspoken language. Take abundant mental notes.

> **QUICK TIP:**
>
> Tell them you're leaving on a certain day but book a Y Class ticket to give you flexibility to change your flight.

Through your liaison, schedule in advance at least a half-hour of free time after meetings. Use this time to capture your thoughts and observations in writing.

### 3 Ways To Detach

> **QUICK TIP:**
>
> Take a step back and just observe what is going on in any person-to-person interaction.

1. See humor in yourself and the situations in which you find yourself. (The word of caution here, of course, is to not allow the humor to show in your face.)
2. Use visualization to gain a more objective and complete perspective on the situation. One such technique is to observe as if through the lens of a camera, changing focus by zooming out for a wide-angle and in for a close-up. Another is to view a situation from the eye of a hummingbird, giraffe or fly on the wall. Some folks prefer the helicopter perspective.

Whatever works to keep you neutral and viewing as a third party.

3. Test your assumptions about what is going on. Filter your interpretations by asking yourself questions: What is he really saying? Is this a case of polite masking shrewd? What is not being said here that—if it were known—would reveal the true meaning of the communication? How do I choose to respond to this situation? Do I need to respond?

Appendix VI shows you how to mitigate ambiguity through documenting your vision in detail.

What are the things that cause ambiguity? Not being able to identify the decision-maker who is holding up the works. Not knowing what previous history enters into the mix. A lack of awareness of how your own actions cause loss of face. A lack of timely, logical flow to the information you seek.

## THE ABILITY TO TOLERATE AMBIGUITY

Most of us are comfortable with new information, as long as it's clear, logical and precise. We can grasp it quickly if it's presented in a linear way.

You will not have that luxury in Asia, where the style of communication is more circular. Information will come at you from many directions almost simultaneously. It will not flow out in linear fashion, but will cycle around, with details being added over time. In the meantime, the situation can remain highly ambiguous.

Ambiguity implies a kind of fuzziness to the communication. There is no clear definition. It could mean one thing; then again, it could mean something else. Who's to say? As a Westerner immersed for the first time in a high-context culture, you can expect a lot of ambiguity. You will not know exactly where you stand because of face issues and surface harmony. Things will be left unanswered, ignored, or covered up. Meanwhile, so much of what's being communicated lies in what's not being said.

Your tolerance for ambiguity will bridge the gap and

make communication a lot easier. Give up your need for instant information and direct responses. Get comfortable with not having all the facts at hand. Accept that eventually things will come together at their own pace.

The ability to tolerate ambiguity will keep you grounded. Although it is not widely acknowledged, it can give you an edge even in our own culture. Good problem solving requires it; otherwise you jump to conclusions too soon. Good negotiation requires it; otherwise you will lose to clever negotiators who have the ability and can use uncertainty as a tool against you. Political smarts require it; otherwise you will fail to see the game that is really being played.

> *"There is so much documentation required that people find it easy to just go along. I didn't want to sign a document because I knew the necessary tests had not been done. On the other hand, it's just PYA. A necessary evil. Someone somewhere needs a signature. [My Chinese colleague] said, 'I have to get this document signed. Once it's signed, we can get on with life and what we have to do.' If I had not signed, all work would have stopped. What's worse?"*
>
> ~ Client, name withheld

### Play It Like Chess

1. You're a novice. Like the game of chess to anyone who doesn't know the rules, a high-context culture appears perplexing and even chaotic at first. Adapt the attitude of a learner. You don't know what you don't know yet. But once you've learned the rules and gained a little experience, patterns will start to emerge.
2. There are classic patterns to the game. This book attempts to explain them: they are trust, face, surface harmony and *guanxi*. With awareness of the game, you can begin to observe how things flow and evolve, how the advantage appears to shift from side to side. As you get good at the game, you will see how to use the patterns to your advantage.
3. Winning the game means knowing that there are many ways to reach your goal. Think several moves ahead. Constantly re-adjust your strategy in response

to the changing information. Keep looking at the big picture and keep an open mind.

### Schedule Down Time

Adapting our interpersonal style, suppressing daytime humor, staying detached, and floating in a sea of ambiguity does not come naturally to most of us. It can wear a person down. Release your tension by taking care of yourself in Asia. Remember, your Asian hosts will have packed a full day of activities for you. Plan in advance and use your go-between to schedule time out.

**QUICK TIP:**

Take care of yourself. Release your tension by going to a fitness club. Have a warm bath after work, before heading off to dinner.

Fortunately, hotels in the commercial areas of the Pacific Rim make that easy to do. They are beautifully appointed and a refuge for the weary traveler. Have a bath or shower after work, before heading off to dinner. Bring your swimming and exercise gear to take advantage of the superb facilities. (There is sometimes an extra fee to use club facilities, which are often open to the local public by membership.) Enjoy a whirlpool, sauna, steam bath or massage. Go to the lounge and enjoy a glass of beer or wine, and relax to the easy-listening music of a piano bar or live band.

# SECRET #16:
# Bring More Value to China than the Competition

**China**

One of my automotive clients travels to China on a regular basis and has great success with his company's venture partner, colleagues and customers. He obviously thrives in the culture. I asked what he does specifically to bring value.

He said, "I look for opportunities to work side-by-side, to explore issues and solve problems. I go with them on the shop floor. When we look under the hood together, I start to see things through their eyes."

## THE POWER OF ONE

His actions illustrate the value a single individual can create through personal involvement. He cares where China is headed. He cares deeply about his customers and local staff. He takes the time to understand the cultural differences, build relationships, and educate them on the importance of quality. That's one person's power to make a difference.

> Position yourself and your company as the partner that will help China meet its dream of prosperity, peace and status in the global community

### Develop Strong Personal Ties

On an individual level, there are a number of ways to bring value. Elsewhere we have discussed the importance of *guanxi* in Chinese business culture. It is important to note here that *guanxi* exists among individuals, not among businesses. Deep respect for authority is vested in the person rather than the

> Stop asking what you can get from China. Ask what you can do to help.

position, in people rather than law. Likewise, loyalty extends to a person rather than to a position, and to a particular manager rather than to the company as a whole. It's all about personal relationships. Any time spent nurturing the relationship will be time well invested.

Do business there long enough and you will become part of the *guanxiwang*—the network of reciprocal obligations. Your personal influence and power will grow as you give them reasons to be indebted to you. At this point, you become a valuable asset within Chinese culture. Who can you introduce your Chinese customers to, in order to reciprocate? What doors can you open for them?

Never take your relationship with local authorities for granted. Since government officials are critical to the success of your venture, your evident commitment to their priorities will open many doors. They are most concerned with long-term sustainability. So, speak to that. Continually seek to win and reinforce their trust in your good will and in the benefits your company brings to all people in their jurisdiction.

- Are your interests aligned with those of your joint venture partner and local authorities?
- What is your plan for transferring technology and management know-how to your partners without losing control of your company's intellectual assets?

> Whereas most Chinese companies are weak in the areas of management, administration and technology, what they do have is more flexible ways of getting things done.

**Value:** If you are being sent to China as an expatriate, insist on cross-cultural training for yourself and your spouse. Learn to say a few words in Mandarin. Acquire basic etiquette (see Part II). Learn about the local history and culture so that you can help your Chinese colleagues build a bridge between past deprivation and future prosperity.

## THE POWER OF THE CORPORATION

When Japan's economy was emerging in the mid-1900s, their strength was their traditional system of management. They proved to be masters at systematizing technology. The Chinese, however entrepreneurial, do not have these strengths to fall back on due to the lingering effects of the old system. Highly bureaucratic management, a lack of quality control, old technology, and untrained management impede progress in China.

Efficiency, productivity, profitability, and high quality were not goals of doing business in State-Owned Enterprises (SOEs). They never had to face a competitive market, never ran out of capital (thanks to government policy), and never needed to find ways to streamline their organizational structures or processes.

That is about to change.

In 2007, the Chinese government will cease to subsidize SOEs. When that reality sinks in, there will be plenty of opportunity to differentiate your company through addressing critical issues that will inevitably arise. I asked Graham Foster, past CEO and author of *The Power of Positive Profit*, what he thought the implications were. This was his reply:

"The Chinese government subsidizes SOEs from 2%–7% and this supports their bottom line, which typically is around 10%.

"In reality, if 7% is going to be removed from your margins, you have three choices: cut your costs, sell a heap more product, or raise your prices. The best solution is to do all three in a balanced way. The sales volume increase depends on the gross profit margin [GPM]. If the GPM is 35%, the sales increase has to be a whopping 20%. This is difficult to achieve in a hurry. To get 7% margin back via cost cutting, the costs have to be reduced by 12%, which is also a tall order. A price increase of 7.5% would work, but will the market accept it?

"The VW [Volkswagen] man, when asked if he can build a Vee Dub cheaper in China than Germany said, 'No way! It's the Chinese Government subsidies that make the difference.'

"So the Chinese economy is faced with some urgent learning on a steep curve. My concern is that many will not take the necessary actions quickly enough and go out of business. We in the West can help educate them quickly."

**Value:**

- How can you help them systematize to improve productivity and cut costs?
- How can you combine the best of what China has to offer with global best practices?
- What tips can you share about how Western companies do business to compete in the global marketplace?
- What other expertise can you share in areas that may not appear to relate directly to your products and processes?

*"Today's Chinese miracle is similar to the Japanese economic miracle of 40 years ago. And until Japanese quality reached world-best quality standards, they had to be content to sell to low ends of many markets. China has to lift its quality in many areas."*

~ GRAHAM FOSTER, CEO, AUTHOR, *THE POWER OF POSITIVE PROFIT*

### Address the Lack of Quality Control

China today grapples with poor quality control and a lack of standardization. They will have to change their manufacturing methods and learn how to balance cost and quality concerns if they are to stay competitive.

From your own company's perspective, this means proceeding with appropriate caution and negotiating for control over quality. Unless you have engineers and resources in China, you have to carefully go through every specification, including both materials and processes.

**Value:** When it comes to quality issues, make a long-term personal commitment to stay the course. Help your colleagues realize the importance of quality in supporting higher prices and moving toward a more market-oriented and open economy. If you have local staff, tie employment security to international competitiveness.

## Understand the Market

> "In North America, the customer pays for the tooling cost, but not in China. We failed to get a contract because we told the customer the tooling fee was a must. Our competition was local and understood the market. They simply amortized the tooling cost into the price and shared the risk."
>
> ~ Xu Baoping, CEO, Siemens VDO Electric Motor (Shanghai) Co. Ltd.

## Address Issues of Face Affecting Customer Service

> "The loss of face culture along with fatalistic religious views works against good customer service. When things go wrong, good customer service requires apology and make good the situation. This is tough for the Chinese culture to swallow. Constant reviewing of everything from the loss of face viewpoint doesn't wash in the rest of the world."
>
> ~ Graham Foster, Director, Pacific Seminars International

**Value:** Train them in current business thinking regarding good customer service.

## Bring Long-Term Perspective to the Table

A frequent complaint is that North American suppliers look for the quick fix. They don't like dealing with personnel changes caused by the frequent promotions and reassignments in Western firms. Venture partners I spoke with suggested that you send staff for two-year assignments.

But a Vice-President of a multinational firm told me that his company never made money in China until they sent their expatriate managers home. It was just too costly in terms of Western-style living accommodations and the need for personal chauffeurs. (If you have been to China, you know it is nearly suicidal to attempt to drive on your own.) Other multinationals have found it costly in terms of burnout and turnover.

If your company does decide to send managers or technical experts abroad, be sure that your Chinese customers know that you are absorbing the cost for the sake of the business relationship. And choose people who have the interpersonal flexibility to thrive in the culture.

And if you want your investment to pay off, send your people for cross-cultural sensitivity training before relocating them to China.

> *"Our research has shown that Asia's 'Best Employers' are those companies which take a longer-term perspective in building their companies and contributing to Asia's competitiveness and growth."*[4]
>
> ~ Philip Revzin, publisher of the *Asian Wall Street Journal* and *Far Eastern Economic Review*

**MILLION DOLLAR MISTAKE #10:**

Not getting cross-cultural training for managers and staff who interact with the customer.

### Find Common Values and Priorities

It is not just your product that the Chinese want; it's what your product will do for the collective good. It's how your product contributes to China's dream of the future. China's goal is self-sufficiency. So the question is, how do you contribute to the dream and make a profit in the process?

***Talk about Vision:***

- Where are you going? Can we help you get there? How can our organizations combine capabilities to get there together?

- How can we work together to solve your problems?
- What value can we create together? How can we work together to provide better value for your customers?
- Which of our products are best suited to the local culture? Which can be adapted?
- How can we help you adapt your product to the global climate and market needs?

As an employer, do not just talk productivity with your local staff. Have conversations about a shared vision. Tie salary increases to performance. Tie performance goals to goals the person wants to achieve for self, family or country.

### Help Them Develop Human Capital

Chances are, you or your Chinese partners have trouble finding and keeping good managers. In fact, the scarcity of trained managers and administrators is a major barrier to China's dream for itself in the new world order. According to a 2003 study by Hewitt Associates, just over 43 percent of senior management in China leave their companies each year. Compare this statistic to 5 percent management turnover in Singapore and 11 percent in Australia, and you understand the unique crisis that Chinese companies face. For expatriate managers, the figures are worse, with 66 percent quitting within 18 months of being hired.[5]

*Fill the Management Gap:*

- When visiting, offer to make a presentation in your area of expertise to work groups or at the local business development center or Chamber of Commerce.
- Discuss your company's strategies for developing leadership from within, succession planning, and performance-based compensation.

- As a company, offer management training to local employees.
- Sponsor business and management programs in Chinese schools and universities.

# SECRET #17: Strategic Negotiation Protects Tiger Lured from Mountains

Westerners tend to underestimate two Chinese truths: the ferocity of price competition and the ferocity of negotiation tactics used against foreigners. The two are connected. Chinese know how to negotiate. They are tough, shrewd and strategic. It's part of their cultural legacy.

### Ancient Wisdom

That legacy includes *The Thirty-Six Stratagems*—a compilation of ancient military maxims, written thousands of years ago. No one knows the author or origin. Originally designed to achieve military objectives, many of these very precise gambits and ploys have been adapted by Western negotiators. Their effectiveness lies in the predictability of human weaknesses, which provide leverage points for achieving an advantage. Think of them as forms of psychological warfare used to undermine an enemy. Some are quite ruthless. Even if you never feel comfortable using these tactics yourself, you should recognize them to defend against them. (See Appendix VII.)

How can you win at a game when you don't even know the rules? And how do you gain respect as a player? Begin with awareness. Knowing the stratagems

**China**

There is huge potential for misunderstanding when negotiating with the Chinese. As others have observed: we think they waste time; they think we waste money. And this is one of the reasons they bargain as insistently as they do—they do not want to be made to pay for Western waste.

Your use of the Working Papers Way to Trust (Appendix VI) will assure a smooth final negotiation and buffer *The Thirty-Six Stratagems.*

will neutralize their power. Guard against human foibles (your own) and tactics (the other party's) that are designed to prey on them. Plan your own negotiation strategies according to what you already know about both Western and Asian mindsets. And control what you can control.

### Lone Tigers Beware

Your first concern is Stratagem #15: "Lure the tiger down from the mountains." It means to bring the enemy out of his lair and into a position of vulnerability. To use another metaphor, the home team always has the advantage. When you are negotiating on Asian turf, you are already in a vulnerable position. You are in unfamiliar surroundings, isolated by language and cultural barriers, perhaps suffering from jet lag.

Away from your sources of strength, you are an easy target if you take the strong individualist, lone tiger role. As in so many situations, Asians draw strength from and negotiate in teams. They are masters at working together to wear their opponents down.

**Strategy:** Don't go it alone. Bring your own interpreter, or you may get only the perspective that the other side wants you to hear. Make sure he or she understands what is necessary to achieve your objective. Let your interpreter both introduce the business topic and make the final comments at the end of the day. They will be invaluable at picking up subtle communication cues. They will protect you from many a negotiation tactic, including the attitude that you are in China now, things are done differently here and you had better adapt.

## PLANNING IS YOUR BEST STRATEGY

In my work in training engineering teams, I notice a marked reluctance to take the time to plan ahead for client meetings. Even when millions of dollars are at stake, they think they can wing it. Yet nothing is farther from the truth. Planning allows you to approach the negotiation from a position of strength.

Furthermore, meticulous preparation is second nature to an Asian business unit. The other side will sense your lack of preparation and your ability to negotiate effectively will be diminished. In order to keep up, you will likely have to spend more hours preparing details than you would do normally.

We are negotiating all the time. Every day, in matters large and small. Many of the communication strategies discussed here apply equally to all of your Asian meetings, discussions and presentations.

### Identify All Interests

Develop a broad set of goals. Be realistic. What is the best outcome you might expect vis-à-vis the worst outcome the other party might realistically accept? Prepare for both best-case and worst-case scenarios.

Determine how your interests and the other party's interests converge. *That* is where you want to focus your strategic planning efforts. It is also a good place to start the negotiation—and to end it. Formulate two or three outcomes that mutually benefit, satisfy and commit all parties. Aim for both sides to win.

Westerners want to compete on the basis of technology and quality and innovation. But to the Chinese, price is the most important component of the deal. They do not seem to be too worried about the rest. They get offended if you want to charge a premium for having a technology your competitor does not have.

**Strategy:** Plan to present solutions, not problems. How much effort are you willing to put into understanding things from their perspective? Ask yourself these questions:

- What do they value?
- What are their long-term interests?
- What are their immediate priorities? (In China, extend this thinking to local government officials and mid-level managers. If you're not helping them to meet their priorities, then your project will not move forward any time soon.)
- What are you willing to do to meet their needs?

### Make No Assumptions

One of the main principles of any negotiation is *make no assumptions*. This is even more true when negotiating with Asians, because there is always so much going on beneath the surface.

Identify any Western business assumptions your plans are based on. Be ready and willing to adjust your thinking as new information becomes known. Otherwise, you may be negotiating on the basis of false assumptions, which can prove disastrous. At the very least, test out your assumptions ahead of time with your interpreter to see if they are valid. Do not assume you understand the other side. Unless you are Asian born and bred, you do not.

> Hide behind the mask of a fool. (Stratagem #27)

And on that topic, do not make any assumptions about who the key negotiator is. You might be surprised at the power of the person who says the least.

**Strategy:** Because of the emphasis on establishing a relationship, Asians will focus on learning about your company before focusing on the agreement. You need to do the same. As much as possible, try to get to know the players on the other team socially before the actual negotiation.

### Send Proper Representation

Count on being outnumbered at the table and don't let yourself be intimidated by their larger numbers. Make sure all the players on your team who should be there are represented.

**Strategy:** Don't be outranked. Plan to have your company represented by someone who holds a position at least equivalent to the highest-ranking member of the Asian team.

- Do not make the mistake of going in without knowing who you are negotiating against. This is critical.
- Ask to meet with the negotiators ahead of time.
- In China, make sure you have identified the Buddha

or main decision-maker. Make sure the Buddha's representative is at the table.

*"I learned that my willingness to give, give, give, give, give, give, give through depth in the documentation, visual artistic impressions, sketches and the like, and regularly scheduled meetings was the key to the trust and credibility. It's like any negotiation: if the logic and reasoning are sound, there's no reason for them to question the content."*
~ KELVIN HUTCHINSON, CEO, VISION IN ACTION PTY LTD. (AUSTRALIA)

### Plan Your Opening Strategy

Asians will ask many penetrating questions, which they will have prepared beforehand. They do this to get you to show your hand first, so they will know your opening position. You need to do the same. Control the negotiation with questions that engage the other party and promote good rapport as well as an exchange of information.

**Strategy:** Ask questions that probe the costs and negative consequences of going with another competitor. Invite opinions based on expertise and experiences. Use a quiet, conversational tone.

### Have Every Detail at Your Fingertips

Prepare cost estimations in detail. Know your profit margins. Know exactly how much you need to receive for your technology in order to stay profitable. Know what you are willing to throw in by way of on-site visits for training and consulting and other peripherals. Put a value on these extras. Make sure your specifications are 100% accurate in every detail. You will lose credibility if there are errors and they will be used against you later. Asians do not tolerate mistakes.

## PLAN FOR CONCESSIONS

*"Grasp the big, let go the small."*
CHINESE SAYING

The final agreement is often a series of concessions. Know in advance what concessions you will be willing to make, to protect yourself from making concessions under duress. Distinguish among those issues and outcomes that are *essential* to your organization (the deal breakers), those that are merely *desirable* (great to accomplish but will not otherwise kill the deal), and those that are *expendable* (these you will negotiate).

- Arrange objectives in priority sequence.
- What lesser items will you compromise?
- What critical items will you not compromise?
- Do alternatives to reaching agreement exist for you?

**Strategy:** Plot out the rate and sequence of the concessions you are willing to make. Which concessions will you hold back to give away when the contract terms get renegotiated during the life of the agreement? (See "Know What a Contract Means in Asia," below.)

### Expect to be Low-Balled

Beat the grass to startle the snake. (Stratagem #13)

The other party's initial position will be far above their bottom line. It is a common tactic in negotiations, and makes use of the fact that people give disproportionate weight to the first information they receive. This phenomenon is called "anchoring." A related tendency: people are more likely to agree to a smaller request if it has been preceded by a larger request.

**Strategy:** Expect a low opening bid so that it won't throw you off. Consider each offer on its own merits, rather than in the context of what has come before it.

### Don't Make Concessions on Future Promises

Interestingly, although trust and relationship are key business components, Asian negotiators have no qualms about taking advantage of a weaker adversary. They may say that they are disappointed that you are not more cooperative. They may threaten to go to the competition for a deal. They may use the silence tactic. Or they may say, "Give me a good deal now and you will get a big contract later."

Be aware that any concessions you make may come back to haunt you weeks, months, or years after the fact.

**Strategy:** Get proof and promise of future business before giving in. Humbly apologize and quietly say, "I'm sorry. That is the best we can do."

**QUICK TIP:**

Making concessions too early in the negotiation signals weakness on your part.

### Don't Make Future Promises in Place of Concessions

Never promise anything you cannot deliver. Your promises will not be forgotten. Forgetting a favor that was extended to you as a concession will be a black mark against you.

**Strategy:** Suggest a short break if the going gets tough. If something comes up that you are not prepared to discuss or comment on, quietly say, "We have not yet thought about that. In order to give you the right information, may we talk about that again in our next meeting?"

### Don't Expect On-the-Spot Concessions

The chances are minimal that in the first rounds you will be speaking with someone with authority equivalent to yours. This opens the way for the other party to refuse to deal with issues by saying they need to consult with decision-makers who are not present at the table. If someone does not have the power, they may not let you know. They will delay and postpone you. When you follow up, they may tell you it cannot be done.

Even when you do meet at last with the person of authority, do not expect that they will match your concessions. It simply may not be possible. If (as discussed in Secret #8) Buddha is not involved, they will have reached their position through a lengthy process of consensus. They will not be comfortable taking sole responsibility for quick, on-the-spot decisions.

**Strategy:** Any change to their strategy means they have to go back to the group for further discussion. Since that is a time-consuming process, your best strategy is to save concessions for which you want concessions in return for the end of the negotiation, rather than asking for a series of concessions throughout the bargaining. That way, the situation gets dealt with once, saving you time, effort and frustration.

### Be Prepared to be Pushed

To catch something, first let it go. (Stratagem #16)

Asian negotiators are masters at telling you at the last minute that they cannot accept your terms to force you to make eleventh-hour concessions. Expect them to push you to the financial, mental and emotional breaking point. Once they know there is no further leeway, they will stop. You will be respected for displaying the Asian mindset and toughing it out.

**Strategy:** When you are at your very (pre-set) limit, quietly say, "This is the best we can do." And be truthful about it.

## CONTROL WHAT YOU CAN CONTROL: TIME

You have agreed to meet on their turf, which immediately puts you at a disadvantage. Don't give away more power by giving up control over the time factor in negotiations. Agree on the schedule and the agenda long before your plane leaves for Asia. Be sure it leaves you enough time to reach your objectives.

### Set a Realistic Time Frame

Unless this is an established relationship, don't plan to seal the deal in one meeting or even one trip. It will take a series of meetings for your Asian colleagues to feel comfortable enough to start to negotiate. The first meetings are often for the purpose of exchanging greetings and establishing a personal footing for the relationship. Attempting to move too quickly contributes to a long, drawn-out negotiation.

Your meeting will involve continuous translation and clarification of each item. This is time-consuming. If you don't account for this factor, you will plan an unrealistic agenda. You will feel intense time pressures and display impatience that could undermine your position.

**QUICK TIP:**

Be vague about when you are scheduled to leave.

**Strategy:** Estimate how much time you think it will take to reach an agreement and then double it.

### Build In a Time Allowance for Stall Tactics

Expect that there will be interruptions, delays and postponements while you are in the midst of the negotiation process. These are all part of "The Stall," a prime negotiation tactic that is especially effective against North Americans, who have a tendency toward impatience.

**Strategy:** To stay in control of the time factor in negotiations, do not commit to a specific departure date. This will disarm the power of "The Stall."

### Don't Get Exhausted at Their Leisure

A busy itinerary can also be a tactic used against you, allowing you precious little time to regroup. Asians have enormous stamina for work and after-hours play. You need to have that same stamina to work through the endless hours of negotiating by day and making merry by night.

**Strategy:** Set aside time in the itinerary for taking care of your own energy level and physical health. Do not allow your company, your customer, your interpreter, or your joint venture partner to book important meetings or negotiations for you within 36 hours of your arrival in the Pacific Rim. You need time to overcome the fatigue of jetlag, which comes with traveling across multiple time zones. Disrupted sleep patterns can cause irritability and loss of concentration at a time when you have to be at your best.

## CONTROL WHAT YOU CAN CONTROL: INFORMATION

The process of negotiation in Asia generally takes longer than in the West and does not follow the same logical process. Issues of price, quantity, quality, delivery, terms, warranties and new technology are not dealt with one at a time. You do not discuss and resolve one issue then move on to the next. Rather, the issues all circulate and intertwine and come up for discussion, seemingly at random. Issues get suspended to the end. Asians deal well with this type of chaos, whereas Westerners tend to lose track. So you are at a disadvantage unless you can adapt to the constant shifts in conversation and suspend the need for clarity and resolution at each stage.

Trouble the water to catch the fish. (Stratagem #20)

### Plan Ahead for Logistics

Prepare a written text of your presentation for your interpreter. At the very least, provide a copy of your notes ahead of the meeting to ensure that nothing is lost in translation. Make enough copies for everyone around the table.

Do not count on the availability of photocopy or printing services in China. Bring at least 20 copies of your written materials (or a portable printer). And avoid using color in your materials since color has such cultural significance.

### Take Copious Notes

Taking notes is the only way to keep track of what both parties have agreed to. Realize that people from high-context cultures have it all over Westerners when it comes to making sense of circular, meandering conversations that appear to lead nowhere. That is why you need to keep meticulous notes of every concession made on both sides. Take the time to review your notes and refresh your strategy as the negotiation proceeds. If this means foregoing a pre-arranged sightseeing trip, so be it. Your first responsibility is the business.

### Document at Each Stage

After the meeting, document the agreement. If the agreement is ambiguous, expect that your Asian counterparts will take advantage of that.

When you negotiate in stages, draw up a memorandum of understanding, signed by all the negotiators, to document agreements as they are reached. This will avoid misunderstandings and save time in the process.

## CONTROL WHAT YOU CAN CONTROL: COMMUNICATION

### Clarify any Misunderstandings

There will be misunderstandings. One problem that may arise is that the other party may not understand the terms of your contract. They will not ask for clarification, out of politeness or embarrassment. Again, enlist your go-between. Thoroughly discuss each point to make sure it means the same thing to both parties, and that both parties agree with each point. Spell out terms and the meaning of the terms. Say the same thing in different words. Do not leave anything open to interpretation. Use simple language. Avoid negative sentences so that you will stand a better chance of being understood. Discuss and come to agreement on every little thing.

### Listen Closely

There is a lot of power in asking, "What do you want?" and then listening for the answer. Listening does not mean agreeing with what is being said, it just means hearing the other person out. Listen with the intent to truly understand, to get inside the other person's model of the world. As the saying goes, seek first to understand, before you seek to be understood.

## More Communication Strategies

- *Keep an eye on the big picture.* Don't get locked into a frame of reference. Ask: In what ways do I have to change my thinking in order to see the big picture?

> *"It doesn't matter if a cat is black or white, as long as it catches mice."*
> ~ Deng Xiaoping (1904–1997)

- *Talk less, say more.* That is the only way to acquire more information than you reveal. Silence is also a potent weapon against Westerners who feel compelled to fill the void with words. Resist the temptation. Either get comfortable with silence or learn to bite your tongue.
- *Do not talk about your deadlines.* Do not give in to the temptation of looking at your watch. Take long, slow, deep breaths to stay calm. Engage yourself totally in the day's events.
- *Beware of easy confidences.* People love to be told things they're not supposed to know. That's the power behind "just between you and me" and "off the record." Use it, but don't get drawn in by it. There is no "off the record" and nothing stays "between you and me."
- *Make your voice communicate kindness.*
- *Watch your language.* Make proposals, not demands.

## Be Realistic about Confidentiality

Do not expect total confidentiality. With the group consensus requirement, all parties need to be informed to reach a good decision. In addition, Chinese are just beginning to recognize the need for confidentiality in business. They will still tell you everything you want to know about your competitor's product and processes and pricing. And your competition will get the same information about you.

## CONTROL WHAT YOU CAN CONTROL: EMOTIONS

Asian negotiators will take advantage of the North American tendency toward impatience and use it to their advantage. Any show of anger, frustration or annoyance will work against you for the same reason. Walking out in a huff is simply not an option. In the unlikely event that Asians display anger, it is merely a tactic to get you to respond. Don't fall into the trap.

Watch the fire burning from the opposite shore. (Stratagem #9)

### Prepare to be Wrong

Don't make the mistake of trying to prove you are right. Drop the ego. Instead of matching wits or showing how much you know, concentrate on achieving your desired outcomes. Focus on how you can make the other party look good within his or her organization. Just as Westerners who represent their labor union in contract negotiations are responsible to their members and have to put on a face for their members, Asians at the bargaining table have to put on a face and account to higher authorities for their results. They need to bargain hard. Let them.

**QUICK TIP:**

Beware the need to prove you are right and to have the last word.

And be prepared that if something goes wrong, they will look to blame the foreigners.

**Strategy:** Make it something other than you, your company or the other party. Give them an external scapegoat: an outside situation, or an idea, or a set of circumstances. Be hard on the problem, easy on the people.

### Prepare for Different Motivations

When you work for a large company, what makes the process of negotiation even more exasperating is the fact that while your own career may hang in the balance, contingent on bringing home the business, your Asian counterpart's career will likely remain unaffected. And consider this: the agreement under discussion may just mean more work for your Asian counterpart, without an increase in pay. Furthermore, in the Chinese scheme of things, you can't make a mistake or lose face if you do nothing. So the person is not as internally motivated as you are to reach a decision.

> The Chinese will keep bargaining until they know you have gone as far as you will go. Even after an agreement has been reached on price, they may try to top off with some extras. This, of course, is when you are at your most vulnerable. Your guard is down when you are relieved that an agreement has been reached. You are tired. You have a plane to catch.

### Be Prepared to Walk Away

In sending you overseas, your company entrusts you with the authority to close a deal. They have made a considerable investment to get you there. You haven't left your family and come all this way to go home empty-handed. Your Asian counterparts know this and will use it to their advantage.

**Strategy:** They have to know that you are prepared to leave without a deal if the numbers are wrong. You can only do that with your company's endorsement. Therefore, your first negotiation is with your own organization.

The solution is to book an unrestricted Y class ticket. You pay full coach fare in return for flexibility and peace of mind.

## CONTROL WHAT YOU CAN CONTROL: HOME OFFICE SUPPORT

Inject realism into your overall strategy when you set out for Asia. Pressure from back home to bag the client and return within a week will only work against you. You may give away too much for the sake of getting the deal sealed before the deadline. Communicate internally within your company about the process and expectations of the negotiation. Establish the goals for your visit. Manage the expectations. Get permission to walk away from the table rather than commit your company to a losing deal. Know that you're not really walking away, but moving the relationship toward a higher order of trust.

You need to be able to go into bargaining with the confidence that you have their full support to leave a bad deal behind.

- Where will you draw the line?
- What is your absolute bottom line?
- At what point will you be willing to walk away, with your company's blessing?

### And If You Reach an Impasse?

> "The key to resolving the impasse is, 'Let's not destroy what we have.' After 20 hours of negotiations in Taiwan, I said, 'Please don't let this happen. When I go back, our whole business relationship will unravel.' Within two minutes, there was a complete reversal. I had exposed my inner core. I asked him as a friend to rethink the situation. He listened."
>
> ~ Joe Varghese, Customer Projects Manager, Motor Division, Siemens VDO Automotive Inc.

## KNOW WHAT A CONTRACT MEANS IN ASIA

Asians do not place the same worth on legal contracts as we do in the West. As Song Jong-Ho of Doowon Group (South Korea) explains, "We really do not value the contract. We just value our word. We are more for friendship than contracts. We don't count on each paragraph. If we understand each other, we can overlook minor problems or differences."

> *"[Asians] really do not value the contract. We just value our word."*
>
> ~ Song Jong-Ho, Director Purchasing, Doowon Group

**QUICK TIP:**

Leave your Western lawyer at home.

### It Isn't the Piece of Paper

Contracts are not part of the traditional way of doing business in Asia and are merely tolerated in the context of international trade. Asian companies prefer general agreements that allow room to maneuver as circumstances change. They would much rather do business on a handshake with people they trust than work from a signed contract.

**QUICK TIP:**

Once you have made a deal, live up to the terms of the agreement.

What is critical is the personal relationship. Asians assume a continuous partnership. There is a sense that when you trust one another enough to do business together, there is no need to document everything. Within China, you will still see business done by spoken agreement, because the bonds of friendship and trust are so strong. Where trust exists, contracts are superfluous. The two companies can talk and come to agreement as needs arise.

You are likely to achieve little more than your bottom line price because of enormous price pressures and competition.

### It's Just the Beginning

Even after the contract is signed, your Asian partners may continue to try for a better deal. One of the fundamental differences between Western and Asian business practices is that to the Westerner, the contract represents the end of the negotiation. The contract is legal and binding. To the Asian, it is just the beginning of an involved relationship.

If you are not aware of this, you might later feel betrayed at what could (mistakenly) look like broken promises. At first, you will think you are hearing decisions and commitments. In fact, the contract is viewed as a statement of intent. As such, it will be considered null and void if it is found to go against the communal good.

And once the contract is signed, the expectation is that, as a trusted partner, you will be willing to renegotiate and accommodate changes to the agreement as required by your partner. When problems arise, you will be there to help them out.

**QUICK TIP:**

Never promise anything you cannot deliver.

Song Jong-Ho explains:

> "We have many bosses—many layers of management and reporting relationships. So it takes a long time to report through the channels. And the person who is responsible for the job is not so clear as you [meaning, does not have the same understanding]. So sometimes, we make a mistake. We say, 'Yes, I will follow your contract,' but I report to my boss, and he wants to amend it. That causes a problem. It's good in that we can discuss and share our opinions, but if it's an urgent matter, it is a problem."

### Promises Mean Everything

Remember, as difficult as getting to agreement may be, getting out of an agreement is equally difficult.

The good news is that your Asian colleagues may drive a hard bargain, but you can trust them to keep their promises. Once you are affiliated with an Asian company, you can expect they will go to extreme lengths to nurture and sustain the relationship. That loyalty is priceless.

*"Chinese are serious about promises but tend to trifle with contracts; foreigners are serious about the contracts but less so on promises."*

~ Yang Jian,
*When Worlds Collide*
CFO China[6]

### Guidelines for the Contract

1. The agreement needs to be clearly written and clearly understood by both parties. If there are ambiguities in

the agreement, you may find that it gets interpreted in their favor. That's just human nature.

2. Separate out each item, and discuss each point separately. Make sure both sides understand one another.
3. Allow time for proper consideration of your proposal. This allows them to show respect for you and your proposal.
4. The contract will get rewritten as it progresses through various layers of approval. Make certain you allow sufficient time for this process.
5. Rather than trying to work out every detail ahead of time, set your mind to the fact that you will discuss matters as they occur throughout the life of the agreement.
6. Negotiations only really begin as the new venture progresses. The real substance of the relationship develops in working through issues on a daily basis.

### Negotiation in China is Never Done.

> "The longer they can keep the negotiation process going by pitting (foreign) competitors against one another, the cheaper the pricing gets. They will get it down to the final two suppliers. As soon as one party walks away, the negotiation is complete. The business is awarded to the survivor. And the negotiation begins again."
>
> ~ Automotive Engineer (name withheld)

# PART II:
# BUSINESS PROTOCOL

# BUSINESS PROTOCOL:
# Know Whether to Kiss, Bow or Go On a Bender

A foreigner's manners and behaviors seem strange and often discourteous to the locals. This is true wherever two cultures collide and is particularly true when West meets East. Our casual style, open manner and frank speech are diametrically opposite to Asian protocol. With so many differences–subtle and not so subtle–between the cultures, there are bound to be misunderstandings and missteps.

Luckily, a little etiquette can go a long way. Respecting Asian traditions will position you as a sophisticated world traveler.

# BUSINESS PROTOCOL:
## First Impressions at Trade Fairs

A senior executive asked me, "What is the best way to make a good impression at a technical fair where you have only 10 minutes with a Chinese person you have never met before?"

In other words: if it takes as long as you say it takes to form any sort of relationship—if you're not supposed to move too quickly and a sense of urgency works against you—and if you don't have the luxury of time, how do you connect with a person in 10 minutes or less?

The good news is that the Chinese, Japanese or Korean businessperson understands the nature of the event and also wants to meet with multiple vendors. So the scene is set for brief connections. You can distinguish yourself by doing a number of small things right:

- Dress well and appropriately and in the finest quality you can afford. (See First Impressions Everywhere, below.)
- Respect protocol, as outlined throughout this section.
- Engage with a slight smile and a polite greeting. Even "hello" is enough. Shake hands or bow. (See "Meeting and Greeting Skills" below.)
- Cut the chit chat. No talk about the weather. No asking about a person's weekend. Asians don't appreciate a lot of small talk. As one Chinese explained the thinking, "You don't know me. That's my business." When you get to the point, people think you know what you're doing.
- Talk confidently. Draw the person into conversation with a question:
  - What brings you to the show?
  - Are you finding what you're looking for at the show?

  - Whether the answer is "yes" or "no" respond with, What are you looking for?

- Do not use humor, as it will have the opposite effect you intend.
- Bring small gifts, such as flags or a memento with your corporate logo. Giving a gift is not only a way to break the ice, but also a way to respect a cultural tradition. Present the gift with both hands.

**QUICK TIP:**

*"Some people would think it isn't important, but to the Chinese, a small gift is a big deal."*

~ Yen Chung, Importer/Exporter

# BUSINESS PROTOCOL:
# First Impressions Everywhere

**QUICK TIP:**

In many restaurants in Korea and Japan, you will be required to remove your shoes on entering. So, save face by wearing clean socks without holes.

### Dress Without Excess

Your good impression starts with what you pack for your trip. Dress conservatively. For men, this means a good quality, dark, well pressed suit. It means shiny black leather shoes and black leather belt, a white or light blue tailored shirt, and a good quality silk tie. Avoid bright colors.

For women, a conservative business suit or dress, flat or low-heeled shoes, and jewelry are good choices. Blouses and jerseys should have a high neckline. Colors should also be subdued.

Jeans are acceptable casual wear, but most Chinese, who are very image conscious, will wonder why you would want to diminish yourself by wearing them. Shorts are not acceptable in public.

### Get the Name Right

We all want others to get our name right. It is a basic need for recognition and respect. Make sure you know the proper sequence of a person's name. What is the first name? What is the family name? Check the pronunciation. Practice saying it. Write it out phonetically. And since it may not be possible as a Westerner to discern by a name whether the person is male or female, check with your contact beforehand.

The structure of names in Asian cultures is different from naming conventions in the West. The surname comes first (unless the person has westernized it for your benefit). Make sure you do not address someone with the Asian equivalent of "Mr. Jim." "Xu Bao-Ping" is "Mr. Xu."

"Zhou Yu-Hong" is "Mrs. Zhou." As a rule of thumb, the Chinese family name is short and usually consists of only one syllable. The given name is often composed of two words, which are sometimes, but not always, hyphenated. However, Chinese are so adaptable that they will often assume an English first name and place it in front of the family name to make it easier for Westerners. For example, my friend Zhou Yu-Hong calls herself Beryl Zhou.

**China**

Refer to your new acquaintances as Mr. Xu or Mrs. Zhou until they tell you to do otherwise. Use the person's first name only after you have been invited to do so.

**Japan**

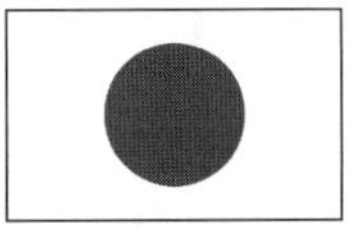

With Japanese names, you can either say Mr. Suzuki, or use the last name followed by "san"—"Suzuki-san."

# BUSINESS PROTOCOL:
# Meeting and Greeting Skills

Make it a point to greet and shake hands with everyone in the room. Both the traditional bow and handshake are appropriate greetings. If your Asian colleague extends a hand, that is your signal to do the same. However, the older and higher ranking the person, the more comfortable he will be with the bow.

### How to Shake Hands

Wait for the other person to extend a hand first. Shake hands, bowing slightly, and state your name and your company's name.

An Asian handshake is typically gentler than the North American handshake. A weak handshake and lack of direct eye contact are not signs of weakness—as you will learn soon enough in negotiation proceedings! But the Chinese shake hands longer than we do. Match the other person's handshake style to build rapport. Your handshake should not be noticeably firmer or friendlier.

**QUICK TIP:**

Expect a gentler version of the handshake. Make yours match the other person's in friendliness and strength.

### How to Bow

With your arms at your sides, allow your hands to slide down the side or toward your knees. Bow from the waist, keeping the back and neck straight. Take your time. Avoid eye contact. How low to bow?

*When greeting someone who is older and wiser or who outranks you:*
Bow lower than he or she does.

*When greeting someone who is your peer:*
Match bows.

*When greeting someone who is your peer and a prospect whose business you want:*
Add an extra bow.

*When greeting someone whose rank you are not sure of:*
Bow a little lower.

*When greeting someone who is below your rank:*
Allow the person to bow lower in order to save face.

## Making Introductions

When someone introduces you, smile and shake hands. Mention the person's name, status and title in your first sentence. For example: "I am happy to meet you, Factory Manager Qian." Make an association to enable you to remember the name in future.

When you are making the introduction, the proper etiquette is to start with the person of highest social status. This may be determined by rank, age or prestige. Since status hierarchies can be difficult to interpret as an outsider, ask your contact to fill you in before the trip about people you will be meeting and the roles they play within the company. Also defer to your liaison's better judgment in the situation.

With each introduction, explain who the person is. Here are examples of how you would introduce non-equals:

- Mr. Song (Director), I would like you to meet Mrs. Strong, who is an Engineer with our company in Germany.
- Mr. Kim (older), I would like you to meet Mr. Lee (younger).
- Mr. Zhang (prospect), I would like you to meet Mr. Henderson (supplier).

When introducing people peer-to-peer, state the name of the person in the customer's company first. For example:

- Mr. Chen (peer in the customer's company), I would like you to meet Mr. Smith (your company peer).

### Meeting Strangers: It Isn't about You

**QUICK TIP:**

If you are applauded as you walk through a factory, the appropriate response is to applaud back.

Asians' gracious politeness is formal and mechanical, and has nothing to do with their true personal feelings about you. Reciprocate in kind. Show courtesy and formal politeness rather than friendliness when greeting. Do not be modest about your credentials and personal qualifications. Make them known from the initial exchange of business cards.

# BUSINESS PROTOCOL:
## Business Cards

In Asian countries, culture and etiquette are deeply embedded in the language. This makes talking to foreigners difficult and introductions awkward for your hosts. The language they use to greet someone depends on where they fit into the regimented social structure. If they do not know where to place you in the social ranking, they do not know how to greet you without perhaps offending. Inadvertently insulting or shaming you could cause them to lose face.

Your business card provides Asian colleagues with the information required to greet you appropriately by establishing your company, position title, rank and credentials. It is an essential part of your image or "package." Have bilingual business cards printed: Mandarin Chinese (gold ink is prestigious) or Japanese or Korean on the one side; English on the other.

Treat your business card with the utmost care. Not only is it critically important to your image, it represents your honor.

### Business Card Exchange

Never throw your business card on the desk or conference table. Since it has your personal and company name on it, treating it casually signifies disrespect for both yourself and the company you represent.

**QUICK TIP:**

There is an art to the exchange of business cards. Practice in advance.

After the bow or handshake, present your card with both hands, which shows respect. Hold it between thumb and forefinger so that it's easy for the other person to read the print. If your card is bilingual—and it should be—present the Asian side.

Receive the other person's card with both hands. Study it for several seconds. Then place it gently on the table in front of you. Do not write on the card.

Do not put it away during the meeting. At the end of the meeting, do not put it into a pocket or wallet or throw it into your briefcase. Rather, place it neatly in your leather cardholder. (Never use plastic because that is low-status.)

To get it right, you need to practice exchanging cards. It's a bit trickier than it sounds to hear oneself being introduced, bow or shake hands, avert the eyes, exchange cards, and absorb information on the card all at once.

Enjoy the ritual. The transfer of business cards is your first chance to get close to your Asian colleague. In the words of my client Joe Varghese, "It's a sincere moment. There are things in life you savor. Make this one of them. Often, this may be your only real contact with this individual."

### South Korea

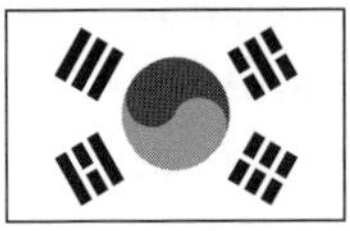

Some Koreans still use Chinese characters on the business card. In the past, it was considered more formal and official. (This is becoming less common.)

# BUSINESS PROTOCOL:
# Gift Rituals

The exchange of gifts is an important part of normal business practice. To an Asian, gifts imply indebtedness. If someone gives you a gift, something will be expected in return. Forgetting about the gift in future would imply ingratitude and make you lose face.

If you give a gift, you may receive a business referral or other form of gratitude in return. Lavish gifts may indicate that a special favor is expected. So keep the value of gifts exchanged appropriate and approximate.

### Come Bearing Gifts

Gifts need not be extravagant. Anything that reflects your company's business or bears your company's logo is appropriate. A carton of cigarettes, a bottle of alcohol, ice wine, stamps, a high quality pen, a paperweight or desk sculpture or other tasteful item which is typical of your city, region or country. (Make sure it doesn't say, "Made in China" or "Made in Japan"!) An expensive cognac or a good single malt whiskey is always well received, although this is changing because liquor is now readily available in Asia. Also, you may find that Asians prefer their own beer or liquor; Western liquor is too strong for the customary heavy drinking during after hours.

> **QUICK TIP:**
>
> If your schedule did not permit time to shop before your departure, pick up a bottle of Scotch in-flight, duty-free.

Bring both corporate and personal gifts. If you are bringing gifts for more than one person, and they share the same rank, the gifts should be the same. A colleague told me that he had brought to a Japanese client a number of company pens in both blue and red. The difference in color caused a flutter of concern, as the recipients attempted to sort out the meaning of the discrepancy. What was the hidden message? Amusing as it was to the Westerner, it was no small matter for the Asians who wondered whether they had been slighted.

### Gifts to Avoid

Gifts to avoid include scissors, knives and letter openers–sharp objects could be interpreted as severing of the friendship or business relationship. Also avoid bringing food gifts if you are invited to someone's home, as that may imply your host cannot provide enough. Sending food–perhaps a fruit basket or expensive candy–as a thank-you gift afterwards, however, is a nice touch.

**QUICK TIP:**

Avoid gifts in quantities of four, which is thought to be unlucky.

Be aware that numbers have significance in Asian cultures. Four is thought to have an unlucky meaning. So don't give gifts in quantities of four. Eight, however, is considered lucky.

### Gift Wrapping

The wrapping and presentation of the gift are often more important than the contents. Have your gifts wrapped by someone local who knows the country's customs. In China, for example, red is a good color for wrapping paper because it means good luck. But in Korea, it means the opposite. In Japan, it's associated with funerals. Gifts wrapped in black or white paper are a definite faux pas. In all Asian countries, white is the color of mourning, and is therefore to be avoided.

### The Exchange of Gifts

When you are offered a gift, let the giver offer it to you two or three times before accepting it. Otherwise, you will appear greedy. Use both hands when accepting the gift. Open it later.

Present your gift with both hands. It is customary for the other person to politely decline the gift. Once, twice or three times. Again, this is part of saving face and giving face. Do not be thrown off. Urge the person to accept. Say, "It's a small thing." Then thank the person for accepting your gift. The recipient will probably not open it in front of you, but will put it aside to open later.

### Gift Giving in China

**China**

In China, pens, watches and day planners are good gifts. Never give a clock, as that is a sign of death. Avoid the color white for the same reason. This includes white flowers.

Exchange gifts after business negotiations are complete. Present the gift to the top person, making it clear that it is on behalf of your entire group and meant for their entire group.

> **QUICK TIP:**
>
> Spending too much on gifts may cause embarrassment and loss of face.

If you admire a thing at a person's home, it may be offered to you as a gift. It would be a mistake to refuse the gift. The thing to do is to reciprocate as soon as possible with an equally valuable gift.

### Japan's Art of Giving

**Japan**

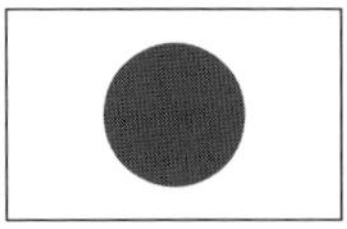

A good Scotch or brandy makes an excellent gift in Japan. Since the number two is said to bring good luck, a pen and pencil set makes a good gift. Or, wrap two bottles of good wine. Beware of lavish gifts from your Japanese counterpart, as it could mean that an equivalent favor will be expected of you later.

To the Japanese, the form and ceremony of the gift exchange are important, not the value of the gifts. Never give an unwrapped gift, as gifts are opened in private. The way a gift is wrapped is so important in Japan that you're best to leave the job to someone else. Have the gift wrapped locally by those who know the cultural significance of the choice of paper and color and adornments. If you must do the wrapping yourself, choose lightly tinted rice paper.

Japanese present gifts at the end of the business transaction. You never want to surprise your Japanese associate. If you present a gift when you first meet, and the other person does not have one to exchange with you, you would cause loss of face. Let the other person know that you will have a small gift to present at the end of your meeting, and allow him or her to present their gift to you first. Expect the response to your gift to be restrained. Subdue your response as well.

**South Korea**

Koreans present gifts at the start of the business transaction.

# BUSINESS PROTOCOL:
# Cultural Celebrations

In any culture, one of the best ways to integrate into society is to be aware of important holidays, their significance, and customary ways of marking them. In Asia, certain holidays afford another occasion for the exchange of gifts.

### Chinese New Year:

**China**

*"Congratulations and Be Prosperous!"*

Chinese New Year is an important occasion. Remembering the occasion helps to forge a strong relationship. Make sure you know the date of Chinese New Year and remember to acknowledge your customer or supplier during this four-day period. The celebration begins on the day of the second new moon after December 22nd, so it falls between the middle of January and the middle of February.

Mark Chinese New Year on your calendar:

| | |
|---|---|
| February 9, 2005 | January 29, 2006 |
| February 18, 2007 | February 7, 2008 |
| January 26, 2009 | February 14, 2010 |
| February 3, 2011 | January 23, 2012 |
| February 10, 2013 | January 31, 2014 |

**QUICK TIP:**

Acknowledge your customer or supplier or local staff every Chinese New Year.

### Happy New Year!

**Japan**

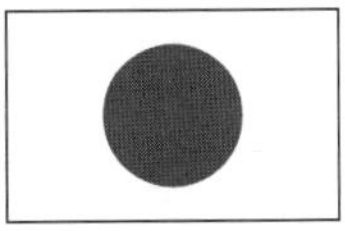

A good time to give a gift is New Year's (January 1st). It is the most important holiday in Japan and lasts for three days. An appropriate greeting is: "Happy New

**QUICK TIP:**

In Japan's big cities, Christmas and other Western holidays are very popular now.

Year! We are deeply obligated to you for your patronage and help last year, and extend our deepest gratitude. We ask that you please continue doing business with us this year." Plan to be in touch immediately after the New Year's celebration.

### Feast of the Lanterns (Obon)

An ancient Buddhist holiday, this is a time when families gather, visit their ancestors' graves, and hold services for friends and relatives who have passed away. Brightly colored lanterns light the way for visiting spirits. Next to the New Year's holiday and Golden Week in late April/early May, this is the most highly traveled time of year in Japan. Government and business offices close for three to five days, July 13–15 (if following the lunar calendar) or August 13–15 (solar calendar).

## South Korea

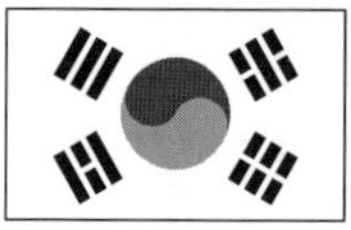

### Independence Day

August 15th is Korean Independence Day. On this day in 1945, Japan gave up dominion over Korea after a 35-year occupation. Unlike Independence Day in America, it is not a day Koreans like to remember. So it's a quiet celebration, without firework displays.

The appropriate greeting is, "Have a happy holiday."

### Christmas Day

Complete with Grandfather Santa, this is a day for exchanging gifts and greetings.

# BUSINESS PROTOCOL:
## The Silent Language

In a high-context culture, even the smallest gesture carries great meaning. And most North American gestures are distracting to the Asian. Knowing the gestures to avoid will earn you respect. Your best strategy is to watch what Asians do and follow suit.

**QUICK TIP:**

Watch and model what Asians do.

### Personal Space and Boundaries

The personal space boundary or "bubble of privacy" of Asians is larger than ours. You will find that, in conversation, they stand farther apart than do most Europeans and North Americans. Touching is an invasion of personal space.

Japanese are more formal than Chinese. They do not approve of male-female touching or shows of affection in public. Men do not engage in back-slapping or other forms of touching.

**Japan**

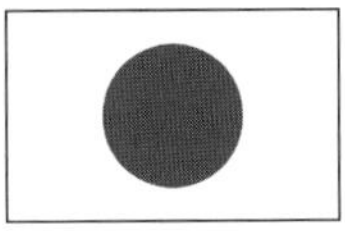

Wherever you are in Asia, best to keep your hands to yourself, or your friendliness will be misunderstood. This applies to all business and social interactions, and not just to the initial introduction.

- Keep your hands off! Do not touch women. Do not touch children.
- Playful backslapping and arm-grabbing are no-no's.

### Crowds in China

**China**

In spite of their hospitality, Chinese do not greet people they do not know with a "good morning" or "good afternoon." The gracious manners are reserved for foreigners, family and people in their inner circle.

The Chinese do not mind touching and jostling in crowds. One shows respect by giving the other person the right of way. This does not apply to rules of the road, however! In actual practice, people push and shove and cut ahead of others who are not members of their circle.

**Japan**

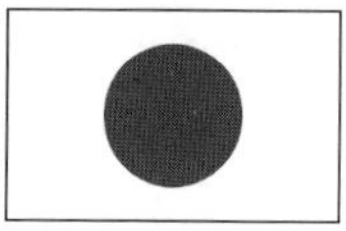

### Making Way in Japan

To get through a crowd, the Japanese may push others. They have a gesture meaning "excuse me," which involves repeating a bow and a karate chop in the air.

### Eye Contact

Direct eye contact is not the norm in Asia. It is seen as disrespectful, even confrontational and hostile. Unfocused eye contact is the norm. So watch that your eye contact is not too direct and intense.

### The Key is Personal Restraint

Asian physical movements are small and restrained, but carry great meaning. Monitor your own facial expressions and physical gestures. Avoid expansive arm and hand movements, unusual facial expressions, or dramatic gestures of any kind.

Some Western gestures convey nothing to Asians. For example, the meaning of the shoulder shrug is lost in translation. The Chinese do shake the head to indicate a negative response, but the Japanese move the open hand, with the palm facing left, in a fanning motion in front of the face. Koreans shake the head or shake the finger left and right, with palm extended.

## Gestures to Avoid

> *"Slouching in your chair, shaking a leg, crossing the knees is showing disrespect."*
> ~ Asian Engineer

Pointing with one finger is considered impolite. Rather, use an open hand. Instead of pointing, wave your hand, palm down, toward the object being indicated, as the Japanese do.

Do not use your finger to call someone over, because it is considered insulting, even when it is done in jest. To beckon "come here," wave the fingers toward your body with the palm down.

## Chinese Sign of Money

Rubbing the thumb, index finger and middle finger together means "money."

**China**

## Japanese Sign of Money

The (North American) "OK" sign means "money" to the Japanese.

**Japan**

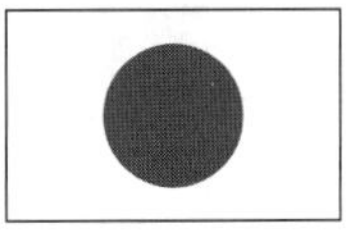

# BUSINESS PROTOCOL:
# The Not-so-Silent Matter of Manners

### Smoking

Smoking is prevalent, and there is not the same concern for degradation of health or the environment. Asians smoke in elevators, on the street, in offices, restaurants, buses and bathrooms. And they do not ask your permission to do so: it is assumed to be okay. If you are a smoker, it is a form of politeness to offer a cigarette and to light the other person's cigarette.

**China**

### Ears, Nose and Throat in China

You may see people blowing their nose between their fingers onto the street. When using a tissue to blow the nose, however, nasal noises are considered bad manners. At the same time, a loud "ah-choo" when sneezing is okay and not frowned upon. Chinese are taught to cover the mouth with a closed hand.

Chinese will clear their throat loudly and often. But they won't spit out. That would be rude. Also, spitting in the streets is now subject to heavy fines. One of my clients who travels to China three or four times a year claims he is used to the throat clearing now, but had a very strong, and negative, physical reaction to it at first.

Belching and breaking wind are not bad manners, but snorting is not allowed.

**Japan**

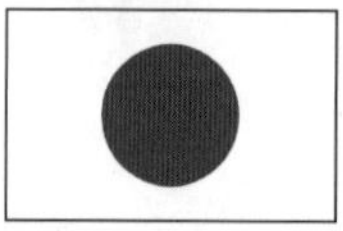

### . . . in Japan

Sniffing, snorting and spitting in the street are acceptable, but nose blowing is not. When you must blow your nose, use a disposable tissue and then throw it out.

The Japanese find the idea of preserving mucus in a neatly folded handkerchief to be grotesque. (Come to think of it, so do a lot of Westerners!)

**. . . in South Korea**

**South Korea**

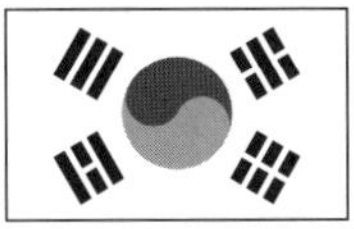

Coughing and nose blowing in front of others are bad manners. And it is extremely bad manners to do so at the table. That's what washrooms are for. On the other hand, burping is quite acceptable to Koreans.

# BUSINESS PROTOCOL: The Business of Entertainment

> *"A long journey tests the energy of a horse. Long days reveal the heart of a person."*
> ~CHINESE SAYING

Asians love to entertain, and you can expect to be entertained on evenings and weekends. Socializing plays a critical role in building trust in Asia, where business is a personal and emotional experience (Secret #9). Eating, drinking, karaoke, and letting your hair down are all in a long day's work.

## TABLE TALK

### Dinner Conversation Do Not's

- Do not talk shop. Business is not discussed during after-hours entertainment.
- Do not assume that all Asians cultures are alike and never make reference in conversation to other ethnic groups. Where we see the similarities, they will see the differences. Chinese culture is older than Japanese culture, and they are proud of that. They are proud of many things. As one of my sources put it: "The Chinese like to think China is the best. Even their dust is the best in the world."
- Avoid talk about World War II and history in general. Resentment of Japan runs deep in China. During WWII, Japan occupied part of China, and that is still vivid in memory.
- Do not talk about backwardness. Chinese are proud of their country's status as the "Middle Kingdom" (center of planet earth).
- In addition, do not discuss Tibet, the one-baby policy or Chinese politics. If the topic of Taiwan arises, refer to it as a province of China and not a country.

### Conversation Do's

- The best dinner conversation is frequent compliments on the food and the meal. Needless to say, it is impolite to take the easy way out and speak English with your colleagues instead of bravely bridging the language barrier.

**QUICK TIP:**

Business practice does not allow for spouses to take part in the evening's festivities.

- Discuss Chinese industrial and economic progress, advances in technology, Chinese arts, and places of geographic interest that you have visited or intend to visit.

### Choose Your Response

People will think nothing of asking you questions we consider highly personal, such as age, salary and marital status. This comes from living in such close proximity and knowing everything about one's neighbors. It is not intended to be intrusive.

Beryl Zhou, who recently moved from China to Canada, explains:

> "The Chinese word for privacy is made up of two characters: 'hide' and 'personal.' The word has the connotation that you have something to hide and are unwilling to share with others. But the word is becoming less negative. People are free not to share personal information about their families with their colleagues. Now, few people will ask your age directly (especially to a woman). However, your age can still be identified by asking which animal symbol you are, because the symbols go in 12-year periods."

If you choose not to reveal the information, give a vague, polite answer, taking care not to cause the enquirer loss of face. For example, if someone asks you a question about your salary, and you do not wish to respond, just say, "It's enough to live on." And if it's a question about age, it's fine to say, in jest, "Oh, I'm still twenty-something (or thirty-something)."

## DINING IN CHINA

### Know How to Host and Be Hosted

If your colleagues invite you to eat, it's high praise, so do not refuse. There is no such thing as "going Dutch." You should be prepared to be either host or guest.

When you are eating out with a group of business people, the most powerful person will usually order for the group, or will delegate that responsibility. As an honored guest, you may be asked if you have a preference or you may be invited to look at the menu. If you are not familiar with the menu, it's fine to say, "Thank you. I trust you to order for me."

When planning a social event around food, keep in mind that most Asians like a sit-down meal. Avoid buffets where people have to line up for food. Similarly, avoid cocktail parties where people stand around, balancing plates of food and drink.

If you are entertaining out, arrive at the restaurant at least a half-hour before your guests. If you are the guest, arrive on time, if not a bit early. As a guest, leave shortly after the meal ends.

**China**

### The Banquet

The evening banquet is the favored form of business entertainment in China. The ritual of the Chinese banquet places a strong emphasis on show of wealth. In reciprocating, you are expected to match the level of extravagance of your host. But make sure not to outdo your host in the amount you spend per person, as this would be an insult and result in loss of face. Spending enough is positive because it shows that you respect your guests and consider them important. It also shows your company's financial stability.

Make sure you have a sufficient budget for socializing or it will hurt your daytime efforts. Not spending enough on the meal signifies you are too poor to afford it, are stingy, or do not respect your guests. If you are stingy, you are not to be trusted.

**QUICK TIP:**

Budget for socializing as part of your business plan.

Expect many toasts expressing friendship, enjoyment and thanks. The host offers the first toast. If you are hosting, prepare toasts ahead of time so that you can keep up. Make them friendly, brief and business-related. Do not drink anything but beer before the first toast. If possible, have a bite to eat before the banquet.

**QUICK TIP:**

Prepare toasts ahead of time.

### Eating in Restaurants

Except for the soup course, you will all eat out of the same pot. You will all be double dipping. You will have no choice. Often, there is no ladle or large spoon that allows you to serve yourself a portion. The food is placed on a revolving tray in the center of the table. The food swings around to you; you help yourself and move it along to the person seated beside you, who helps him or herself and so on. You may be served one dish for every person at the table.

**QUICK TIP:**

Select a good Chinese restaurant and confirm with your guests that your choice of restaurant is acceptable to them.

### When You are the Guest

**Figure 2.1**

Seating Hierarchy

- Do not be seated until you have been shown where to sit.
- Table seating is arranged according to hierarchy. The host (1) usually faces the door or entrance and sits directly across from the guest of honor (6). Strategically, the position facing the door allows the host to control the events. It frees him to look after meal logistics without constantly disturbing the conversations of honored and higher status guests. It allows the host to greet guests as they arrive, and see them out at the end of the evening. However, as the guest of honor, you may be given this superior position.
- Those who have higher status by reason of age or position flank the host, with the most prestigious of the two seated to the right of the host (2).
- The interpreter (7) sits to the right of the honored guest (6).

**When You are the Host**

**Figure 2.2**

Seating Hierarchy

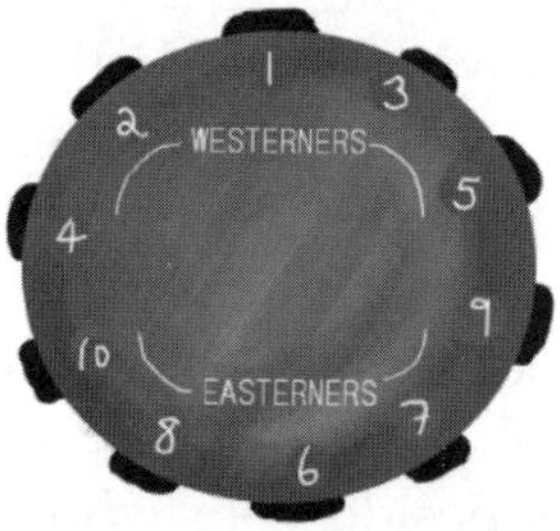


**QUICK TIP:**

When you are the host, make place cards to indicate where people will sit.

- Protocol requires that you confirm with your guests that your choice of restaurant is acceptable to them.
- Even selecting the right restaurant has to do with face. So when entertaining Chinese guests, picking the right restaurant is important.

- Keep Chinese and guests separate, or they will feel very uncomfortable. Using a familiar seating arrangement makes your guests feel at ease and saves face.
- Use the services of your interpreter to guarantee that you do things right.

## CHINESE TABLE ETIQUETTE

**QUICK TIP:**

Always leave food on your plate.

In Chinese entertaining, it is a traditional courtesy to fill the guest's plate with food so long as the guest continues to eat. This custom is best understood in the context of China's long history of scarcity and famine, combined with warm hospitality and a preoccupation with face. Custom also requires that the guest continue to eat. As you can imagine, this can make for interesting situations.

### The Art of "Enough"

Since finishing what is on your plate signifies you are still hungry, the practice is to leave some food on your plate. Similarly, taking any food remaining in the serving dish signifies you are still hungry, and that is an insult to the host. At banquets, if boiled rice is served near the end of the meal, and you eat some, that signifies that you are still hungry and your host was not generous enough. If you finish your entire plate (as we are accustomed to doing in the West), your host will feel shame because it is a sign you are still hungry, or did not like the food. This leads to loss of face on the part of the host. Leaving a bowl full is also considered rude.

It is impolite to ask for a second cup of tea or coffee, or to help yourself to a second cup. When you do not want any more beverage, leave some in your cup or glass.

### Eat and Don't Ask

It is bad manners to refuse food. Eat a bit of everything. At least make the appearance of moving it around on your plate. It is good manners to sample every dish. If you do choose to decline food, be very gracious about it. Do not ask what you're eating. Sometimes, ignorance is bliss. (Do you really want to know you are eating scorpions or bear paw soup?) Do not let surprise, disgust or displeasure at the sight of the food show on your face.

Your host may honor you by placing choice morsels on your plate—with his chopsticks, of course! If this is upsetting to you, do not let it show. (Then again, if he is following protocol, he will be using the large end of his chopsticks to serve you with.) Passing along the last few bites of the preferred dishes (often the meat dishes) to the host is considered good manners.

### Wait to Eat

It is considered rude to start to eat or drink before others. Wait for the eldest or highest ranked person to begin to eat. In fact, it is good manners to start eating only after your host has urged you to begin.

### Don't Wait to Leave

Do not expect desserts, although fresh fruit may be served at the end of the meal. When fruit is served, that signals the meal is ending. You are expected to leave once the meal is over, and to leave before your hosts.

### Eat, Burp and Be Merry

Slurping your soup is a good thing. So is eating noisily and burping often. They all mean you enjoy and appreciate the meal.

Toothpicks may be provided. It is considered polite to clean your teeth with a toothpick at the table, but only if you cover your mouth with your free hand and try to look inconspicuous by turning your face away from your dinner companions. It is not good to show your teeth.

One of the quaint Chinese customs is that the messier the guests leave the tablecloth, the greater their satisfaction with the meal. For that reason, an older, more traditional Chinese restaurant may not provide napkins. You may want to carry a package of moist towelettes in case you find yourself in that situation.

## CHOPSTICKS

Most people are familiar with chopsticks. They are long, thin rods that taper slightly at one end. The narrower end comes into contact with the food.

In restaurants, as in homes, chopsticks and a soupspoon are the only cutlery provided. You will receive only one set for the entire meal. Koreans are the exception here—they use a spoon to eat soup and rice.

**INTERESTING FACT:**

Even the size of a family's chopsticks reflects status in China: the thinner the chopsticks, the higher the status.

### Chopstick Etiquette

Use chopsticks to pick up chunks of meat or vegetables from your plate or soup dish. Secure the food so that it does not fall off the sticks in transit to your mouth.

Also use your chopsticks to eat rice or noodles. Scoop the rice into your mouth, without your teeth touching the chopsticks. (The contact of the chopsticks with your mouth or teeth should be minimal.) Hold the bowl close to your mouth when eating. Or move your head close to the bowl. Your left hand should hold or touch the bowl when you eat (or the reverse for left-handers). It's okay to slurp your noodles.

When not in use and when you are done, place the chopsticks beside your plate on the tablecloth. Do not leave them on the bowl. Never stick the chopsticks straight up in the rice, as this is a sign of aggression and disrespect. At the very least, it is not polite. If a chopstick rest is provided, place the tapered end of the chopsticks on the rest.

**QUICK TIP:**

Unlike in the West, reaching in front of others to serve yourself from the serving bowls is quite acceptable.

**A Chopstick How-To**

**Figure 3.1**

1. The bottom chopstick rests between the base of your thumb and index finger. Your fingers point toward the narrow end of the chopstick.

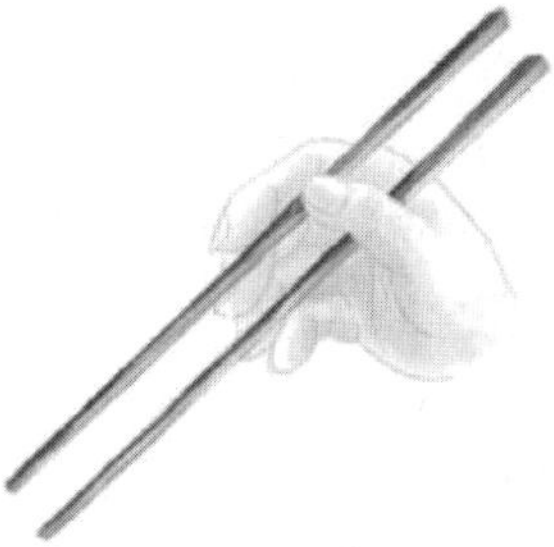

**Figure 3.2**

2. Hold the top chopstick between your index and middle fingers, secured by the upper half of your thumb.

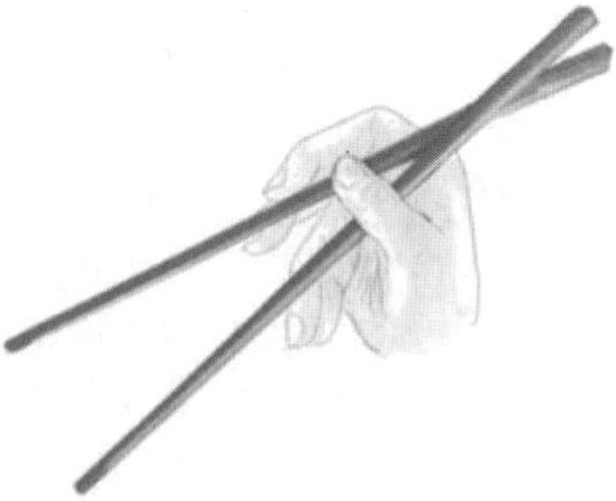

**Figure 3.3**

3. Only the top chopstick moves. The tips of the thumb, index, and middle fingers control it like pincers or tongs to grip the food in a claw-like motion. The ring finger balances the bottom chopstick while your index finger does most of the work.

## Chopstick Serving Etiquette

If serving chopsticks or spoons are provided, use them instead of your own chopsticks. If not, then use the thicker end of your chopsticks to transfer food from the serving dishes to your own plate or bowl. Never transfer food directly to your mouth from the serving dish.

It is bad manners to pick and choose and poke around with your chopsticks for a tasty morsel. You are expected to choose from what is on top and to select what you want before reaching for it. Once touched, it is yours, and goes directly to your plate.

## Chopstick No-No's

Needless to say, although Westerners may find many interesting and creative uses for chopsticks, they are to be used strictly as eating utensils. Do not use them for pointing, gesturing, catching attention, skewering food, or moving dishes closer. Do not lick or suck on the tips. Do not click the bowl or otherwise make noise with your chopsticks.

It is considered bad luck to drop your chopsticks.

# BUSINESS PROTOCOL:
# Social Drinking

A special, more profound relationship results when you join in the heavy drinking cultures of the East. It's a matter of trust. Asians believe you don't know a man until you have spent time with him drunk.

Refusing to drink is socially gauche. If you have a problem with alcohol for any reason, politely let your host know that you are unable to imbibe. Your Asian colleagues will understand if you give a medical reason. Otherwise, your not drinking will be regarded with suspicion. What do you have to hide?

### Drink Pouring Protocol

In the Asian world of drink, you never drink alone and you never fill your own glass. Even the host does not fill his own glass. You pour the host's drink. Someone else will fill your glass.

As with everything, there is a glass-filling hierarchy. The general rule is that the glass of the person with the highest seniority gets filled first. The junior person pours for the more senior person. If the more senior person fills a lesser mortal's glass, that is an honor indeed.

Since it's bad manners to pour your own brew, it's good to know how to hold the glass while beer is being poured for you:

- Lift your glass and cradle the bottom of the glass in your left hand, wrapping the fingers of your right hand around its circumference.
- Slant your glass toward the person filling it.
- Say, "Thank you."

### Toasting

Toasting is an integral part of business dinners and evenings out. The host offers the first toast. In parts of China, you honor your host by lowering the rim of your glass when clinking a toast.

Here are some popular toasts that mean "Cheers!":

**Cantonese:** *Yum-sing*

**Mandarin:** *Kam-pay*

**Japanese:** *Kan-pai*

**Korean:** *Gun-bae*

### Imbibing Tips

Be aware that your Asian hosts might make a little game of testing your drinking prowess. How much can you drink before getting totally bombed? The trick is to eat something before you drink. Do not go to a banquet on an empty stomach. Strong tea helps to counteract the alcohol.

If you're not a drinker, small sips are fine. The interesting dimension of surface harmony means that it is perfectly acceptable to take little sips and act drunker and happier than you are. As long as you keep drinking, the glass keeps getting filled. The way to refuse a drink is to quietly say, "No, no, no" (sounds like one word, "*nonono*") and give some excuse. Otherwise, just leave your glass untouched and that will signal that you are done.

**QUICK TIP:**

Be happy. Be merry. And don't think too much about what others drink.

**QUICK TIP:**

Never pour your own drink.

### Drinking in China

The need to drink and keep pace with your drinking prowess is not as stringent in China as in Japan and South Korea. "People like you more when you are involved, but won't dislike you if you

**China**

don't drink," explains my friend Beryl Zhou. "Usually people think that you respect them when you accept the offer to drink. However, if you can't drink or can't drink too much, that is fine. The business will still go on."

The favorite liquor is *bai jiu*, which tastes rather like diesel fuel and compares favorably to Buckley's Mixture.

**Japan**

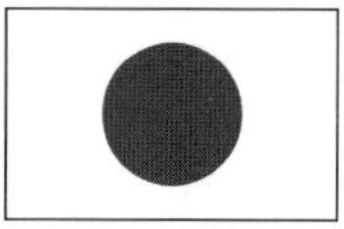

## Entertainment in Japan: Strictly for the Male of the Species

Entertainment in Japan includes heavy drinking parties. Ritualistic drinking goes back to religious practices from centuries ago.

Entertainment may include the company of geishas. Men may be asked if they want a woman for the evening.

Since clients have asked me how to refuse an offer without causing loss of face, I asked a Japanese friend. This was his response: "If you do not wish to participate, thank them for their warm gesture and politely decline. If they persist, say you are married and happily as well. The pressure may be high but they'll respect you in the end. The perception of 'faithfulness' is not necessarily the same between the East and West. Being entertained with Geisha is a cultural experience in itself and I don't think there is anything wrong with it. I would just be firm as to where I draw a line if more than a friendly level of hospitality is offered my way, whether at a Geisha house or any other place offering various types of entertainment."

**South Korea**

## No Driving Under the Influence

After-hours drinking also plays an important role in Korean business practice. But the drinking is less frequent and a bit less excessive. (Or so say my Korean friends! Certainly, the signing of an agreement or contract calls for an evening celebration.) Koreans like to go home to their families in the evening. So while you will be treated to lunch in their guest facilities, you will be on your own at night unless work extends into the evening hours.

Whereas Japanese people use the subway, Koreans prefer to drive their own cars to work. The "do not drink and drive" law is strongly enforced in Korea, and has had an impact on the amount of liquor consumed.

# BUSINESS PROTOCOL: Kara-oke!!!

The appeal of Karaoke has everything to do with providing a psychological release valve in a culture that otherwise restricts the show of emotion. As Beryl Zhou explains,

> "Karaoke is very popular in China. We Asians don't often have a chance to show our emotions. We were trained to be quiet, cover and package ourselves, and develop an image. Karaoke allows us to show emotions to others. To some degree, it's a chance to show off.
>
> "Normally, senior bosses are serious and not often joking. Through joking and laughter, we can develop deeper relationships with colleagues and customers."

## No Way Out

You will be expected to participate. One of my clients tried to insist that he could not join in. English was not his first language, he pleaded, and therefore he did not know the lyrics. His Asian colleagues graciously accepted his excuses that night. However the next evening, true to their reputation as excellent hosts, they presented him with the lyrics of songs in his native Spanish tongue. Now there could be no excuse for him not to join in. This tells you something about the quality of Asian hospitality and the importance they attach to their bonding and merrymaking.

## Musical Anchors

You may have noticed that not everyone likes the same music. The music of our youth has the greatest emotional impact on us. We resonate to those tunes of our teen years throughout our lifetime.

So when you want to connect with someone at an emotional level, play the music of their adolescence. And know the lyrics too! This is especially important in business relationships, where you can expect your hosts to be of an older generation. They will appreciate the older tunes, not just the current pop hits. I have read that *Red River Valley* has particular appeal because the melody is almost identical to an old favorite Chinese folksong. Other older Western tunes that you may hear include: *Amazing Grace, I've Been Working On The Railroad, My Bonnie Lies Over The Ocean*, and *Swing Low, Sweet Chariot*. Other simple "folk" tunes include *Country Roads* and *Moon River*. (For assistance with the lyrics, see Appendix VIII, Karaoke: Your Folksong Repertoire.)

*"Folk songs tend to be popular with the older group to build relationships. There is a deeper meaning in the songs and memories of the past, when they were younger. The themes of hardships and triumphs are similar on both sides of the ocean."*

~ JOHN LIANG, P. ENG., MOTOR DIVISION, SIEMENS VDO AUTOMOTIVE INC.

**QUICK TIP:**

Knowing the lyrics to a few older songs will endear you to your Chinese hosts.

### Back to the Grind

It is an interesting paradox that, in spite of the fact that business is a personal experience for Asians (Secret #9), they do make a distinct separation between business and pleasure. When the singing is over and the dawn comes, it will be down to serious business as usual in the boardroom. No matter how heavy the hangover, you are expected to be there, looking sharp and on the ball. I know of at least one instance where a young engineer's career was permanently stifled because he failed to show up for a morning meeting after a night of heavy drinking.

**QUICK TIP:**

Drink and be merry, but get thee to the shop on time.

# APPENDICES

# APPENDIX I:
# First Time Travel to China

## YOUR PACKING CHECKLIST

China

- Warm woolens (If visiting during the winter, factories will be cold, especially in the north.)
- Walking shoes
- Money belt
- Facial tissue
- Toilet tissue
- Moist towelettes
- Prescription medications (in their original containers)
- Vitamins (in their original packaging)
- Intestinal antiseptic (such as Bio citrus, a concentrated lemon seed extract)
- Personal hygiene products
- Eye drops (in case of dust storms)
- Echinacea (To ward off cold infections, also try Yin Chao.)
- Basic first aid supplies to treat minor injuries and prevent infection in an emergency: antibiotic towelettes; soap; adhesive tape or bandages; sterile dressings; Q-tips; antibiotic ointment; antiseptic solution; eyewash solution; and perhaps a pair of sterile gloves.

### Bring a Carry-On

My client Joe arrived in Asia two days ahead of his luggage. He had to wear his traveling jeans in business meetings the next day. This is simply never done in the East, and caused him great unease. Adding insult to injury, he spent several frustrating hours shopping for overpriced golf shirts, socks and under things. The lesson learned: always carry a spare set of clothing and essentials in your carry-on, in the event you and your checked-in baggage do not arrive at the same destination.

**QUICK TIP:**

Wear business attire on the plane. You don't want to be stuck in blue jeans if your luggage doesn't make it through.

## IN PREPARATION

Normally your Chinese customer or supplier will meet you at the airport. If this is not the plan, have your Chinese contact send you written directions to your destination. While the person who directs you to your taxi at the airport will speak English (see below), it is unlikely that the driver will understand your instructions. The actual Chinese characters are probably better than the Pinyin spelling.

If your plans include visiting a plant or going to a customer's office, have your customer fax you a business card with the address destination. You may want to ask how much you might expect to pay for the taxi ride from your hotel.

## EN ROUTE

### Travel Reservations

If you have a joint venture (JV), get your JV partner to make your airline and hotel reservations. You will save about 50% on fares and room rates. In Shanghai, they can book you a 5-star hotel for USD $75 a night. The corporate room rate at the deluxe Shangri-La Hotel (posted on the Internet at $210–$230) may be as low as $90.

### Air Travel

Try to book your flight on Japan Airlines (JAL). Their rates are reasonable and the food is great. You get overnight accommodations and breakfast at a fine Japanese hotel en route to China. All of this will minimize the inevitable discomfort of travel.

### Customs and Immigration

In the larger centers, customs and immigration counters are modern and easy to locate. Just follow the signs. If the lineups are long, go to an outside line, preferably one beside a booth that serves dignitaries and airline staff. When free, they will signal you to pass through. And you will save time.

Have all your paperwork completed and ready to hand over with your passport.

### Getting to the Hotel

Most hotels will pick you up at the airport if you notify them ahead of time. If you do not have someone meeting you at the airport, you are well advised to take a taxi, and not a private driver service, no matter how official the person looks who wants to lure you into a private car.

Find the actual taxi stand, and you will be guaranteed a controlled price. Legitimate taxi drivers will not be there to solicit you as you exit to the street. An employee of the taxi company will direct you to your taxi.

If you do choose to go with a private car, make sure you negotiate the price before walking too far. (By the time you get to the far reaches of the parking area, you may feel it's too late to change your mind and you're too tired to make the effort.) You could end up paying three or four times the going rate.

When you check in at the hotel, ask for the hotel's business card. It will have a little map that will direct your taxi driver to make sure you get back again without undue expense or irritation.

## JET LAG

### Insomnia? Disorientation? Take Melatonin

Right off the bat, you lose a day when you arrive in China. For many people, travel across several time zones means your internal clock gets turned around. On your return, it can take from two to three weeks to fully recover from your trip. It can make you cranky and less productive. Melatonin is one way to counteract the negative effects of air travel on getting a good night's sleep.

In the United States, melatonin is readily available across the counter. It can also be ordered online. As with any nutritional supplement, consult your physician before use, especially if you have a known condition or are on other medications.

### *Heading to Asia*

The idea is to sleep when the people at your destination are sleeping, and not during meetings. (Yawning is just one more way to cause loss of face.) Take the prescribed melatonin dosage between 6 p.m. and 7 p.m. (*your time*) on the evening of your flight to Asia. Take one dose at bedtime (*local time*) the evening of the day you arrive. Ditto for the next four evenings.

If you are traveling further east into another time zone, take a dose the day before you travel, again between 6 p.m. and 7 p.m. (*local time*) and repeat the above procedure.

### *Heading Back Home*

Take one dose of melatonin at bedtime (*local time*) the day you arrive home and for the next four evenings. If you happen to wake up during the night, take another half dose to get a full night's sleep.

### *Either Direction*

You will arrive at your destination feeling better if you keep yourself hydrated on the plane. Forget the alcohol. Drink lots of water and fruit juices. That will give you an excuse to get up and stretch your legs. Splash water on your face when you visit the facilities and use lotion liberally if your skin tends to dryness.

### *Jet Lag Prevention*

The alternative to Melatonin is Gastrolyte®. While Melatonin restores sleep patterns, Gastrolyte® treats dehydration, which also contributes to jet lag. It stimulates intestinal water absorption and is used to correct fluid loss and electrolyte imbalance. My sources tell me it is the preferred remedy of jumbo jet pilots.

Gastrolyte® is an over-the-counter effervescent flavored tablet made by Rhône-Poulenc Rorer Pharmaceuticals, Inc.

*"Gastrolyte® is an over-the-counter tablet similar to most dissolvable effervescent tablets. Pop it in a half glass of water and drink. I just got back from London, England. Took two and I feel fine today."*

~GRAHAM FOSTER, DIRECTOR, PACIFIC SEMINARS INTERNATIONAL (REGULARLY TRAVELS FIVE CONTINENTS)

### *Jet Lag Recovery*

The rule of thumb is that it takes a day for every hour of time difference to recover from jetlag. If there is a 12-hour time difference between China and your home, it will take 12 days to recover from your trip. Unless you take the above precautions.

## CURRENCY

All cash transactions are in Renminbi (RMB), which is fixed to the US dollar. At time of writing, the exchange rate is USD 1: 8.28.

The old Yuan still circulates but businesses would rather take the RMB to avoid fake currency. The 50-Yuan note is a popular counterfeited item. The RMB offers more security.

When you exchange cash or travelers' checks, keep your receipts. You may be required to show proof of your payment before you can convert back to your currency. This policy was established to discourage black market currency speculation.

### Credit Cards

Foreign credit cards are accepted in larger hotels. Generally they are not accepted at stores or restaurants. For cash advances on major credit cards, you can go to a bank with your passport, but expect to pay a premium service charge.

### Interac

You will not see Interac outside major cities. ATMs in certain cities are connected to the Chinese banking system only.

### Travelers' Checks

Most merchants do not accept travelers' checks as direct payment for items or services. You can cash travelers' checks at your hotel, and will get a better exchange rate there than at a bank. There is a nominal, flat fee. You will get a better exchange rate on travelers' checks than on cash.

## SECURITY

Since cold hard cash is the only widely accepted currency, you will be carrying around quite large sums of it. Bring a money belt and keep all cash on your person.

### Hotel Security

Hotel staff sometimes enter guest rooms at will, often without knocking first. Their job is supposedly to prevent theft and keep out those who have no legitimate business in foreign-resident compounds, but the general consensus among most foreigners is that security guards are also there to keep an eye on them and their activities, and to report any suspicious goings-on.

Despite this coming and going, there is very little crime against visitors in China because the penalties for crimes against foreigners are so severe.

In four- and five-star hotels, your room will have a safety deposit box that is large enough to hold your laptop. Or you can use the hotel's safe.

**QUICK TIP:**

*"Use a Hotmail account when you are in a foreign country. Otherwise, you may spend days removing a virus from your system — like I did."*

~ Gerry Murak, Murak & Associates, LLC

## FOOD & RESTAURANTS

A Western or Asian breakfast is included with your accommodations.

Eating is China's national past time. Many people do not have kitchens where they live, and so they eat most of their meals in the street.

Hotels are multinational and you will have no problems ordering from the menu.

Otherwise, if you are eating out and are not with someone who speaks the language, select a restaurant that displays an English menu or photos of their selections. Some places have different dishes on display so you can point to what you want to order.

### Comfort Food

In the large centers, you will find all the major fast food chains, including Subway, KFC, McDonald's and Pizza Hut. They are easily recognized because they bear their familiar corporate identities. But who wants to fly halfway around the world to eat familiar fast food when superb Chinese cuisine is available everywhere?

### Hygiene

Since the SARS outbreak of 2003, you will see handwashing stations in fast food restaurants. In open kitchens, the servers wear masks and rubber gloves.

### Hydration

*Green Tea*

Drink green tea made with boiling water to stay hydrated if you have doubts about the water.

**QUICK TIP:**

Stick to boiled, pasteurized and fermented drinks to avoid getting sick while you're away.

*Bottled Water*

Never drink the water unless you see the bottle being cracked open in front of you.

*Warm Soda*

Soda is served warm, unless you request that it be served cold. Forget about diet cola (or ice) at restaurants outside the major hotels. You should skip the ice, in any case. If you are diabetic and require artificial sweetener, bring your own.

**FASCINATING FACT:**

*Tsingtao* Beer, China's first beer brewery, was built by German investors in 1903 in Qingdao, a major coastal city in east China's Shandong Province. *Tsingtao* is one of the most famous brands in the world.

*Great Beer*

No country in the world brews more beer than China. Expect to pay two or three times more for imported beer than Chinese beer. But why would you do that when there's *Tsingtao*?

*Tipping*

Except perhaps at some of the major hotels in commercial centers such as Shanghai and Beijing, there is no tipping in China.

## GETTING AROUND

### Take a Taxi

**QUICK TIP:**

The Chinese word is "*taxi.*" The word "cab" is not understood.

Taxis are inexpensive. Take taxis everywhere, rather than renting a car. You can reserve or hail one at restaurants and hotels. Fares (which are posted) differ according to the car model. Have someone at your hotel write your destination in Chinese to avoid confusion and to ensure you get to business meetings on time.

In bad weather, or at rush hour, if there is a line-up for taxis you do not stand a chance. People will butt in ahead of you.

### Traffic Hazards

Road conditions outside major centers are horrendous and best left to local drivers. People drive their cars the way they used to ride their bicycles—in the wrong direction, on sidewalks, and over the curbs. With the proliferation of car sales in China, combined with the rural exodus to the cities, traffic congestion will get worse before it gets better.

### *Whose Turn is It, Anyway?*

The turning vehicle has the right of way, whether turning right or left. The vehicle that is going straight has to stop. Vehicles wanting to change lanes do so when they are just inches ahead of another vehicle, so cars are constantly jockeying for position. Sometimes, they even come to a full stop at a red light.

### Walking? Riding the Bus? Be Wary

Pedestrians are expected to yield the right of way to cars and bicycles. Sidewalks are not safe either. Cars do not slow down for you. Drivers lean on their horns and spare their brakes. Bicycles are often moving against the flow of traffic.

If you are riding a bus, look to your right as you get off the bus. Cyclists, who ride between the curb and the bus, often don't stop for exiting bus passengers.

Hitting a foreigner means heavy fines, and that's a deterrent. Nonetheless, take care of yourself and make sure you can be seen. If you need to cross a street without the assistance of a traffic guard, attach yourself to a group of locals. As I once heard, *"If you hear a bus horn honk behind you, ask not for whom the bus honks—assume that it honks for thee."*

## SHOPPING

### Labor-Intensive Purchases

At some of the larger department stores and pharmacies, you select your purchase and leave the item with the salesperson, who writes up a ticket on rice paper. You take the ticket and go elsewhere to pay for your purchase. The system is cumbersome, but—as with so much else in China—the rationale is that it guarantees employment for more people.

## Scratch 'n' Win

There is a scratch and win portion on your receipt that looks like a lottery ticket. The government did this as an incentive to promote businesses to write receipts and to encourage patrons to take the receipts.

## Negotiating Price

Always negotiate price in advance. That applies to merchandise, restaurant meals and taxis (unless metered). Failing to do this will result in paying a lot more than the going rate. Unless you are shopping at a Century-Mart or Wal-Mart, you can pretty much negotiate price.

## Negotiating with Street Vendors

As soon as you step out of a taxi into a market or shopping area, vendors will approach you. They will invite you to follow them to their homes to buy fake Gucci handbags, Louis Vuittons, Omegas, Rolexes and DVD's. Politely say, "No thank you." My Chinese sources tell me that locals never buy from street vendors. So consider yourself warned.

If you do choose to bargain, tell them you want to see the best quality. Know that the wily street vendor will try to sell you the junk first. Your best strategy is to walk away, but not too fast. The vendor will chase you down. If he does not chase you down, and you want the article, just walk on by later, slowly. He will remember you and start haggling again.

There are four stages of negotiation:

1. Outrageous price (for example, 600 RMB for a fake Rolex watch).
2. Outrageous counter-offer. (For example, 100 RMB.) They will scream like you've stolen their first born child.
3. "For you, you're my friend, best price."
4. If he walks away cursing and swearing, you've insulted him. But that is soon forgotten and does not

mean he won't still haggle with you later. But be warned: he may switch the product or try to give you change in the old Yuan. Do not accept it. Only Renminbi (RMB) is accepted since 1994.

### The Barbershop Experience

For a man, getting a haircut in China is truly a sensual experience. It addition to a shampoo, it includes a scalp, back, arm and finger massage. As part of the feel-good experience, you will have your fingers cracked and your ears cleaned with Q-tips.

Barbershops are open all night long. And there is a good reason for that: they are fronts for prostitution. The brightly lit shops are more overt in their pandering. Expect to be solicited. Pornography and prostitution are illegal, and it's best not to get involved.

## IF YOU GET SICK

If you need medication and can self-diagnose, you can walk right into a pharmacy and purchase what you need off the shelves, without a prescription. The pharmacist will guide you. Pharmacies are indicated by a green circle with a green cross.

**QUICK TIP:**

You may want to look into AirMed Assistance, an annual membership that provides prepaid hospital-to-hospital international air ambulance transportation. http://www.airmedassistance.com

## CULTURE SHOCK!

Expect culture shock to set in right away. Crowds are rude and pushy. And people in the state-run shops and restaurants tend to display bad manners, as though you were an interruption to their day.

Forge onward nonetheless. The further you stray from your hotel, the deeper you will get into Chinese customs. Your every effort to assimilate into their culture will be rewarded. It helps tear down walls and warms the day-to-day work relationships.

### Language Barrier

Purchase a soft-cover paperback English-Chinese dictionary on arrival at a major airport. They are bulkier but quicker than electronic versions. English is spoken at all major hotels.

### Get the Numbers Right

Learn to count to 10 in Chinese (see Appendix II). But don't count on being understood even if you master the higher numbers, because the pronunciations are easy to confuse. You'll be saying one thing and they'll be hearing another. Using hand gestures won't always work because they may mean something different than intended. Who would have known, for example, that the outstretched thumb and forefinger would stand for eight? Your best strategy to avoid confusion is to put the numbers in writing.

### Things to Not Let Yourself Get Upset About

*Jostling:* As with driving, jockeying for position occurs wherever there are lineups. It is not considered rude, and, once again, being at the head of the line has to do with status. It's just the way it is, so get used to it already.

*Noises and Smells:* Food in the streets. Throat noises. Adjust.

*Public Restrooms:* The Chinese use the European abbreviation for "water closet" (WC). So if you need to use public toilet facilities, write "WC" and they will know what you mean.

*Lack of Home Comforts:* There is no toilet paper in public areas. Bring your own tissue. Pack and carry with you some moist towelettes in the event you go to an older Chinese restaurant that does not provide napkins with the meal.

*Uncomfortable Requests:* Be wary that some people you meet will want to use their new friendship with you, not just to practice their English skills but also to solicit your help in securing a travel visa, an opportunity to study abroad, or a job in a joint venture. If you do not wish to oblige, simply lower your eyes and apologize profusely that this request is "impossible at this time."

## GUESTS WELCOME

Westerners traveling to China have a decided advantage. If you come from any distance, you will be treated well and will receive a warm, hospitable welcome. Taking good care of foreign guests is part of the Chinese culture. It is expected. You will find that they are very generous people who will go out of their way to help foreigners.

You may get stared at. This is due to the influx of people moving from rural areas to find work in the major centers. Some people you come across will never have seen a Westerner. Expect that, when you get off the beaten path, little children may come up and want to touch you to see if you are real.

### Friendship and Respect

Respect for an individual extends to their entire family. By virtue of friendship with one member, you are welcomed into the entire clan. (Interestingly, the Chinese word for "family unit" is the same as the word for "circle.")

### Honor and Prestige

If you get invited to visit a colleague's home, do not refuse. You honor them with your visit. They welcome the opportunity to show themselves at their best.

*"The thought process goes like this: When you come into my home, you brighten it and make it feel better, more. If important people come to my home, my neighbors will respect me. You give me prestige and help me gain respect."*

~ Yu-Hong (Beryl) Zhou, P. Eng, Siemens VDO Automotive Inc.

# APPENDIX II: Useful Mandarin Words, Phrases and Numbers

Chinese characters are symbols that represent an idea or object. Since there have never been official pronunciations, the sounds associated with the Chinese characters differ depending on the dialect spoken. To complicate things, China has seven major dialects and 80 spoken tongues.

The Pinyin system of using the Latin alphabet developed in China in the 1950's to simplify communication. Pinyin pronunciations are based on Mandarin tones, as Mandarin is the official language of government, education, and business in Mainland China. (The language of business in Taiwan is Mandarin. The language of business in Hong Kong is mainly Cantonese.)

## Pinyin Pronunciation Guide to the 23 Pinyin Letters

*17 Familiar Sounds:*

| Letter | Pronunciation | Letter | Pronunciation |
|---|---|---|---|
| B | As in **b**ay | N | As in **n**ay |
| Ch | As in **ch**urch | P | As in **p**ay |
| L | As in **l**ay | Sh | As in **sh**irt |
| M | As in **m**ay | G | As in **g**o |
| S | As in **s**ay | F | As in **f**at |
| K | As in **k**it | Y | As in **y**es |
| D | As in **d**ad | H | As in **h**it |
| W | As in **w**ay | T | As in **t**ime |
| J | As in **j**eep | | |

*6 Unfamiliar Sounds:*

Fortunately, there are only six letters that do not correspond to English pronunciation.

| Letter | Pronunciation | Letter | Pronunciation |
|---|---|---|---|
| Q | As in **ch**eer | Zh | As in **j**ump |
| Z | As in rea**ds** | X | As in **sh**e* |
| R | As in leis**ure** | C | As in ha**ts** |

* thinly sounded

## Useful Mandarin Words and Phrases

| English | Pinyin Spelling | Pronunciation |
|---|---|---|
| Hello | Ni hao | Nee-how |
| Good morning | Zao | Zow |
| Good afternoon | Ni hao | Nee-how |
| Good evening | Ni hao | Nee-how |
| Good night | Wan an | Wan an |
| How are you? | Ni hao ma? | Nee-how-mah |
| Very good | Hen hao | Hun-how |
| I am pleased to meet you | Hen gao xing jian dao ni | Hun-gow-sheeng-jeean-dow-nee |
| Goodbye | Zai jian | Zai jeean |
| Please | Qing | Ching |
| Thank you | Xie-xie | Sheeuh-sheeuh |
| You're welcome | Bu keqi | Boo-kuh-chee' |
| My name is | Wojiao | Woa-jeeow |
| I'm from | Wo shi cong … laide | Woa shi tsong … la-ee duh |
| I'm lost | Wo milule | Woa meeloo luh |
| I'm sorry | Duibuqi | Dooy boo chee |

| English | Pinyin Spelling | Pronunciation |
|---|---|---|
| Where is the ... | ... Zai nail (reverse word order) | ... zai nah lee |
| Could you help me? | Ni keyi bang wo ma? | Nee kuh yee bang woa ma? |
| How much? | Duo shao qian? | Dooa shao cheean? |
| That's too expensive | Tai guile | Tai gooy luh |
| I would like | Wo xiang yao | Woa sheeang yow |
| Airport | Fei ji chang | Fay jee chang |
| Hotel | Jiu dian (or) Fan dian | Jeeoh deean |
| Restaurant | Can ting / Fan dian | Tsahn ting / Fan deean |
| Store | Shang dian | Shang deean |
| Hospital | Yi yuan | Yee Yooan |
| Pharmacy (Western Medicine) | Xi yao fang | Shi yow fang |
| Pharmacist | Yao ji shi | Yow jee shi |
| East | Dong | Dong |
| West | Xi | Shi |
| South | Nan | Nan |
| North | Bei | Bay |
| Street | Jie | Jeeuh |
| Road | Lu | Loo |
| Lane | Xiang | Sheeang |

## Numbers

| Number | Pinyin Spelling | Number | Pinyin Spelling | Number | Pinyin Spelling |
|---|---|---|---|---|---|
| 1 | Yi | 11 | Shi′ yi | 21 | Er shi′ yi |
| 2 | Er | 12 | Shi′ er | 22 | Er shi′ er |
| 3 | San | 13 | Shi′ san | 23 | Er shi′ san |
| 4 | Si | 14 | Shi′ si | 24 | Er shi′ si |
| 5 | Wu | 15 | Shi′ wu | 25 | Er shi′ wu |
| 6 | Liu | 16 | Shi′ liu | 26 | Er shi′ liu |
| 7 | Qi | 17 | Shi′qi | 27 | Er shi′qi |
| 8 | Ba | 18 | Shi′ ba | 28 | Er shi′ ba |
| 9 | Jiu | 19 | Shi′ jiu | 29 | Er shi′ jiu |
| 10 | Shi | 20 | Er shi′ | 30 | San shi′ |
| 31 | San shi′ yi | | | | |
| 100 | Yi bai′ | 1000 | Yi qian′ | 10000 | Yi wan′ |
| 200 | Er bai′ | 2000 | Er qian′ | 20000 | Er wan′ |
| 300 | San bai′ | 3000 | San qian′ | 30000 | San wan′ |

| | |
|---|---|
| 1 million | Yi bai wan |
| 10 million | Yi qian′ wan′ (1,000 ten thousands) |
| 100 million | Yi yì (pronounced (ee–*ee*) |
| 1 billion | Shi yi (one billion is ten one hundred million: 10 yi) |

# APPENDIX III: Embassy Contacts in China

## AMERICA

**American Embassy in Beijing**
3 Xiu Shui Bei Jie
Chaoyang District, Beijing, People's Republic of China
Telephone: (86-10) 6532-3431
Fax: (86-10) 6532-4153
Email: AmCitBeijing@state.gov

**US Consulate General in Chengdu**
No. 4 Lingshiguan Road
Chengdu, Sichuan, 610041, People's Republic of China
Telephone: (86-28) 8558-3992, 8558-9642
Fax: (86-28) 8558-3520
Email: consularchengdu@state.gov

**US Consulate General in Guangzhou**
No. 1 Shamian South Street
Guangzhou, 510133, People's Republic of China
Telephone: (86-20) 8121-8000
Fax: (86-20) 8121-9001

**U.S. Consulate General in Hong Kong and Macau**
26 Garden Road
Hong Kong SAR
Telephone: (852) 2523-9011
Fax: (852) 2845-1598

**US Consulate General in Shanghai**
1469 Huai Hai Zhong Lu
Shanghai, 200031, People's Republic of China
Telephone: (86-21) 6433-6880
Fax: (86-21) 6433-4122

**US Consulate General in Shenyang**
No.52, 14 Wei Road
Heping District
Shenyang, Liaoning, 110003, People's Republic of China
Telephone: (86-24) 2322-1198
Fax: (86-24) 2322-2374
Email: shenyangacs@state.gov

## CANADA

**Canadian Embassy in Beijing, Consular Services**
19 Dongzhimenwai Dajie
Chao Yang District
Beijing, 100600, People's Republic of China
Telephone: (86-10) 6532-3536
Fax: (86-10) 6532-5544
Email: bejing-cs@dfait-maeci.gc.ca

**Canadian Consulate in Chongquing**
Suite 1705, Metropolitan Tower
Wu Yi Lu, Yu Zhong District
Chongqing, 400010, People's Republic of China
Telephone: (86-23) 6373-8007
Fax: (86-23) 6373-8026
Email: chonq@dfait-maeci.gc.ca

**Canadian Consulate General in Guangzhou**
Suite 801, China Hotel Office Tower
Liu Hua Lu
Guangzhou, 510015, People's Republic of China
Telephone: (86-20) 8666-0569
Fax: (86-20) 8667-2401

**Canadian Consulate General Shanghai**
604, West Tower
1376 Nanjing Road (West)
Shanghai, 200040, People's Republic of China
Telephone: (86-21) 6279-8400
Fax: (86-21) 6279-8401
Email: shngi@dfait-maeci.gc.ca

## AUSTRALIA AND NEW ZEALAND

**Embassy of Australia in Beijing**
21 Dongzhimenwai Dajie
Beijing, 100600, People's Republic of China
Telephone: (86-10) 6532-2331
Fax: (86-10) 6532-6718

**Australian Consulate General in Guangdong**
Room 1509, Main Building, GITIC Plaza
339 Huanshi Dong Lu, Guangzhou
Guangdong, 510098, People's Republic of China
Telephone: (86-20) 8335-0909
Fax: (86-20) 8335-0718

**Australian Consulate General in Hong Kong**
23/F Harbour Centre,
25 Harbour Road
Wanchai, Hong Kong SAR
Telephone: (852) 2827-8881
Fax: (852) 2585-4457

**Australian Consulate General in Shanghai**
Level 22, CITIC Square
1168 Nanjing Xi Lu
Shanghai, 200041, People's Republic of China
Telephone: (86-21) 5292-5500
Fax: (86-21) 5292-5511
Email: acgshang@public.sta.net.cn

**New Zealand Embassy in Beijing**
1 Ritan Dongerjie
Chaoyang District
Beijing, 100600, People's Republic of China
Telephone: (86-10) 6532-2731
Fax: (86-10) 6532-4317
Email: nzemb@eastnet.com.cn

**New Zealand Consulate General in Shanghai**
Qi Hua Tower, 15A

1375 Huai Hai Road (c)
Shanghai, 200031, People's Republic of China
Telephone: (86-21) 6471-1108
Fax: (86–21) 6431-0226
Email: nzcgsha@uninet.com.cn

## UNITED KINGDOM AND EUROPE

**British Embassy in Beijing**
Floor 21, North Tower,
Kerry Centre
1 Guanghualu,
Beijing, 100020, People's Republic of China
Telephone: (86-10) 8529-6600 x3303
Fax: (86-10) 8529-6081
Email: consularmailbeijing@fco.gov.uk

**British Consulate General in Chongqing**
28/F Metropolitan Tower, Zourong Road
Chongqing, 400010, People's Republic of China
Telephone: (86-23) 6381-0321
Fax: (86-23) 6381-0322
Email: Bcgchq@public.cta.cq.cn

**British Consulate General in Guangdong**
Guangdong International Hotel
339 Huanshidong Lu
Guangzhou, 510098, People's Republic of China
Telephone: (86-20) 8335-1354
Fax: (86-20) 8331-2799
Email: guangzhou.consular@fco.gov.uk

**British Consulate General in Shanghai**
Suite 751, Shanghai Centre
1376 Nanjing Xilu,
Shanghai, 200040, People's Republic of China
Telephone: (86-21) 6279-8130
Fax: (86-21) 6279-8254
Email: consular.shanghai@fco.gov.uk

**German Embassy in China**
17, Dongzhimenwai Dajie
Chaoyang District,
Beijing, 100600, People's Republic of China
Telephone: (86-10) 6532-2161
Fax: (86-10) 6532-5336

**General Consulate of Germany in Shanghai**
14th Floor, New Century Plaza
188 Wu Jiang Lu
Shanghai, 200041, People's Republic of China
Telephone: (86-21) 6217-2884, 6217-1520
Fax: (86-21) 6271-4650, 6218-0004
Email: info@gk-shanghai.org.cn

**Note:** The information in Appendix III and Appendix X is correct at time of writing. Please send changes to china@chinainmotion.com.

# APPENDIX IV: Chamber of Commerce Contacts

## AMERICA

**The American Chamber of Commerce, PRC**
China Resources Building #1903
8 Jianguomenbei Dajie
Beijing 100005, People's Republic of China
Telephone: (86-10) 8519-1920
Fax: (86-10) 8519-1910
Email: mjf@amcham-china.org.cn
Website: www.amcham-china.org.cn

## AUSTRALIA

**Australian Chamber of Commerce in Hong Kong**
4/F Lucky Building, 30 Wellington Street
Central, Hong Kong
Telephone: (852) 2522-5054
Fax: (852) 2877-0860
Email: austcham@austcham.com.hk
Website: www.austcham.com.hk

## BRITAIN

**British Chamber of Commerce in Beijing**
3I Technical Club, 15 Guanhuali, Jianguomenwai
Beijing 100010, People's Republic of China
Telephone: (86-10) 6593-2150
Fax: (86-10) 6506-5231
Email: director@pek.britcham.org
Website: www.britianinchina.com

**British Chamber of Commerce in Hong Kong**
Room 1201, Emperor Group Centre, 288 Hennessy Road
Wanchai, Hong Kong
Telephone: (852) 2824-2211
Fax: (852) 2824-1333

Email: Info@Britcham.Com
Website: www.Britcham.Com

**British Chamber of Commerce in Shanghai**
17-01/02 Westgate Tower, 1038 Nanjing Xi Lu
Shanghai 200041, People's Republic of China
Telephone: (86-21) 6218-5022, 6218-5183
Fax: (86-21) 6218-5066, 6218-5193
Email: membership@sha.britcham.org
Website: www.britcham.org/sh

## CANADA

**Canada-China Business Council, Beijing Office**
Suite 18-2, Citic Building, 19 Jianguomenwai Street
Beijing 100004, People's Republic of China
Telephone: (86-10) 6512-6120
Fax: (86-10) 6512-6125
Email: ccbc@public.gb.com.cn
Website: www.ccbc.com

## EUROPE

**European Union Chamber of Commerce in China**
Office C316, Lufthansa Center, 50 Liangmaqiao Road
Beijing, 100016, People's Republic of China
Telephone: (86-10) 6462-2065
Fax: (86-10) 6462-2067
Email: euccc@euccc.com.cn
Website: www.euccc.com.cn

**German Chamber of Commerce in China**
Landmark Tower II, Unit 0811
8 North Dongsanhuan Road
Beijing 100016, People's Republic of China
Telephone: (86-10) 6590-0926
Fax: (86-10) 6590-6313
Email: germanchamber@ahkbj.org.cn
Website: www.ahk-china.org

# APPENDIX V: How to Find a Trusted Intermediary (For the Entrepreneur)

## There are Two Ways to Find an Intermediary[7]

**1. The More Traditional Route:** Contact your country's Consulate in Beijing, Shanghai, Guangzhou, Chongqing, or Hong Kong (and perhaps there are more in other provinces or regions). If they understand what you are trying to accomplish, they will give you leads and links to associations (or their equivalent) or to Asian business-people who have expressed an interest in wanting to do trade with Westerners. Also contact local Chambers of Commerce (see Appendix IV).

**2. The Less Traditional Route:** Start communicating with the Asian community in a major Western center. Befriend people. Spend time burning the boot leather: walking, talking, befriending, shooting the breeze. Spend time, money and effort. "I'm in (type of business). I'd like to buy you coffee/lunch/dinner." (Be as generous as you can afford to be.) Treat them in a friendly manner. Subtly, and with care, talk to them about what you are trying to do. Then keep them as part of your network.

They will point you in the right direction, and, if sufficiently westernized, will do so without too many strings attached. They will introduce you to a contact with the right fit. The reason they will be interested is the potential benefits to them. Just knowing someone and introducing the person will give them social status.

You will need the names of about 12 people to whittle down to a manageable three or four people to interview.

**10-Step Due Diligence Process:**

*From Home*

**Step 1:** Have your new contacts open the way with introductory emails to their connections in China.

**Step 2:** Contact each person by email. Refer to the third party introduction. Give a brief background on yourself. Be totally upfront about your intentions. "May I send you an outline of what I am trying to do, along with my personal background and my business? And will you in turn let me know about your network and how we might be able to work together in your country?"

**Step 3:** Send more complete information on yourself, your company and your objective. In one brief paragraph, outline what you want to achieve (without giving away the farm). For example:

> *Pharmaceuticals:* My aim is to manufacture pharmaceuticals for export, with a potential turnover of USD $50 million.
>
> *Property Development*: I want to develop integrated resorts valued at USD $60 - $100 million. Locations are open at this stage.

**Step 4:** Allow them a few days to digest your message. They will likely go discuss it with others in their clan.

> "What is important is the initial documentation you send in, because the first question their network is going to ask is, 'Will these people make us look good and will they make us wealthy?' They will not ask you this information. They will not say this to you. They have to be able to determine your bona fides, your sincerity, and your ability to do what you say."
>
> ~ Kelvin Hutchinson, CEO, Vision in Action Pty Ltd. (Australia)

**Step 5:** Based on the replies you receive, select three or four contacts to pursue in China. Let them know when you plan to arrive, and when you would like to meet with them. By the time you get on the plane, you should be 70% comfortable that any one of the three or four might be your leverage point in China. Bring small gifts, out of respect for cultural traditions.

*In China*

**Step 6:** Now you have to do due diligence on each person you have selected. You do this very tactfully. Allow two days and one evening per person. You cannot risk the relationship. The first half-day is the "getting to know you" phase. During that time, you do not talk business. It's a process. It's a ceremony. It's a dance. Put the time and effort into building the relationship at this stage, or you will have problems.

> *"The time and effort you put into your intermediary is what will get you the ultimate deal."*
> ~ Kelvin Hutchinson, CEO, Vision in Action Pty Ltd. (Australia).

**Step 7:** Then you have to rely on your instincts and business skills to make the judgment that this is the group, team, or network that you want to start building a longer-term relationship with.

**Step 8:** Keep two of the relationships going for three or four months.

**Step 9:** Then select one and keep fostering the relationship with the chosen partner.

**Step 10:** Find a palatable way of concluding the deal with the parties you have not selected, without losing face on either side. Refer to something they said, a condition, or issue they raised earlier that led to your decision. Let them know that the situation is insurmountable. "This is something we cannot live with. I don't think that we can proceed because that seems to be something that would make a deal impossible to pursue." Be as concerned with your ethics as you would be at home.

# APPENDIX VI: The Working Papers Way to Trust

Working Papers form a critical part of an evolving business plan or model. They allow you to document your vision and provide a framework for building buy-in through a *shared vision*. Each paper revolves around a specific idea or topic that provides the critical information the middle person or intermediary needs to engage in behind-the-scenes preparations for discussion with the main decision-maker or Buddha.

This method protects face, because it ensures detailed understanding of your concepts and business plan. Sound logic and reasoning will guarantee a smooth negotiation. There will be no reason to question the content or your intentions, as you will have provided the blueprint in stages.

## How to Develop Working Papers

Prepare each document as a stand-alone file, with background, rationale, analysis and logic built into the text. Write clearly, using plain English text. Use visuals at every opportunity, including sketches, charts, diagrams, and artist impressions to appeal to the visual bias of many Asians. Create a visual brochure of the concept. For some projects, consider presenting the paper in a brochure format.

Keep the subject documents short and sweet. Depending on the topic, the length may vary from one paragraph to five pages. Your goal is to gain trust through removing all ambiguity from the communication. Comprehension is critical. Transparency builds trust.

## How to Present Working Papers

Plan an approach that allows sufficient time for your

intermediary to understand and absorb information at each stage. Pacing is important: allow your Asian colleagues a week or two to translate, discuss, process and form questions around each paper.

### Create a Sense of Ownership

Although you are the one doing the documenting, you want others who are involved in the project to feel that they are a part of its evolution. When presenting the papers, invite feedback and respond to their questions in writing.

### Suggested Working Papers Topics[8]:

1. Background
2. Topic Description
3. Issues to Consider
4. Alternatives Considered
5. Critical Success Factors
6. Costs Involved
7. Staffing Requirements
8. Regulatory Considerations
9. Risk Assessment
10. Strengths, Weaknesses, Opportunities and Threats (SWOT)
11. Cash Flow/Feasibility (if required)
12. Timeline
13. Rollout Considerations
14. The Next Step
15. Recommendations

> *"Not documenting the vision is the number one reason deals fail in China."*
> ~ Kelvin Hutchinson, CEO, Vision in Action Pty Ltd. (Australia)

Save your Working Papers on a server or in a central location (not just on your personal computer) so all parties can access the file. Working Papers become your company's intellectual property.

### How to Deliver the Working Papers

Deliver the Working Papers in a staged process. Face-to-face is important. Deliver the papers in person.

> "What I learned to do when I went to Asia, was to take things step by step. I flew in regularly, to give them a week to think about the document I had left with them. I spoke about the document I had left behind at the end of the last meeting. 'What did you think of . . . ?' 'What are the questions from the Working Papers that I delivered at the last meeting?' I would embrace most of their ideas because that was their buy-in and their ownership of each facet of the rollout of the project. Then, with some ceremony, I would deliver the next range of Working Papers and would then expect them to translate, discuss, process and form questions around them for the next week.
>
> "Whether the project was a property development, theatre restaurant or information technology concept, this is the process I used."
>
> ~ Kelvin Hutchinson, CEO, Vision in Action Pty Ltd. (Australia)

# APPENDIX VII: The Thirty-Six Stratagems (Interpreted)

**1. Cross the Sea under Camouflage.** Act up-front and enthusiastic about a project and co-operate readily. This will deflect suspicion away from your true, darker motives.

**2. Besiege Wei to Rescue Zhao.** Don't focus your energy on your opponent's strengths. Instead, attack where he's weakest or most vulnerable.

**3. Kill with a Borrowed Sword.** When you know you've met your match, send someone else to do the dirty work.

**4. Await the Exhausted Enemy at Your Ease.** Bait your opponent into bickering over issues that mean very little to you. When he's worn down by the small stuff, you will still have energy for the real fight.

**5. Loot a Burning House.** The best time to negotiate is when the other side is desperate—be it from internal strife, falling markets, or cash flow. They won't have time or energy to negotiate properly.

**6. Pretend to Attack in the East, Attack in the West**. Start by fiercely negotiating issues of little worth, suggesting they have more meaning to you than they do. Then suddenly, reverse directions and address the points that really matter.

**7. Create Something from Nothing.** Bluff once, they will believe you. Bluff twice, they will believe you. Bluff three times, they will begin to doubt you. That's when to attack.

**8. Openly Repair the Walkway but Advance to Chencang by a Hidden Path.** Plan a double attack to divide your opponent's attention and energy. One is head-on, the other is indirect. Both converge on the same points and same goals. (Think "good cop, bad cop" tactic.)

**9. Watch the Fire Burning from the Opposite Shore.** Let the players around the table wear each other down while you watch. Once they show signs of fatigue, go in with your full strength.

**10. Conceal a Dagger in a Smile.** Ingratiate yourself in order to earn trust, meanwhile secretly plotting against an opponent.

**11. Sacrifice the Plum for the Peach.** Sacrifice short-term objectives and benefits to achieve long-term goals. Someone has to be your scapegoat for the greater good of the group.

**12. Grab a Goat in Passing.** Stay flexible and open to every new opportunity as it arises, no matter how small.

**13. Beat the Grass to Startle the Snake.** Launch a mini-attack and step back to observe your opponent's reactions and behaviors. This will help you to form your strategy against him.

**14. Borrow a Corpse to Raise the Spirit.** Recycle an old idea, method, or technology and adapt it for your new purpose.

**15. Lure the Tiger Down from the Mountains.** Bring the enemy out of his lair and into a position of vulnerability—cut off from his sources of strength, be they family, friends, familiar surroundings, colleagues or home office support.

**16. To Catch Something, First Let It Go.** Let your opponent believe there's still hope, even when there is not, and rally around it. When he discovers the truth–that there is no hope–it will crush whatever is left of his morale.

**17. Toss Out a Brick to Attract Jade.** Lure your opponent, using visions of wealth and power as bait.

**18. To Catch the Bandits, First Capture their Leader.** Assess the loyalty to leadership within your opponent's company. If it is weak, then you're safe to attack the leader head-on. His underlings will soon join you.

**19. Steal the Firewood from Under the Pot.** If your opponent is bigger and more powerful, avoid a direct confrontation. Instead, identify the sources of his power and work away at those.

**20. Trouble the Water to Catch the Fish.** Make your opponent vulnerable by distracting him with a strange or unexpected action. He will become more focused on your unusual behavior than on his own strategy.

**21. Shed Your Skin Like the Golden Cicada.** When all signs point to retreat, first create an illusion or distraction to draw attention away from your escape.

**22. Bolt the Door to Catch the Thief.** When you can see you've backed your opponent into a corner, finish it there. Don't give him a chance to regroup.

**23. Befriend a Distant Enemy to Attack One Nearby.** It is easier to make allies among those who are separated by distance, size, or status, since "familiarity breeds contempt."

**24. Borrow the Road to Conquer Guo.** Use an ally to attack a common enemy. Then, turn against your ally using his own resources and strategies against him.

**25. Replace the Beams and Pillars with Rotten Timbers.** Change the rules of engagement to confuse your opponent and disrupt his strategies.

**26. Point at the Mulberry But Curse the Locust Tree.** When the situation does not allow you to confront an opponent directly, proceed with passive aggression, innuendo and analogy. Your opponent will be helpless to respond directly.

**27. Hide Behind the Mask of the Fool.** Play the fool so that the opponent doesn't perceive the real threat of your abilities and knowledge.

**28. Lure Your Enemy onto the Roof, Then Take Away the Ladder.** When the bargaining really heats up, cut off all communication channels and keep your opponent negotiating without breaks.

**29. Put Silk Blossoms on a Dead Tree.** Present a worthless point, technology, or asset as very valuable.

**30. Exchange the Role of Guest for that of Host.** Feign weakness, act co-operative, and resign to playing on their turf. The strategy is to gain trust and insider access, so that you can learn more about your opponent's weaknesses.

**31. Send a Beautiful Woman as Decoy.** A beautiful woman will distract the men and cause internal competition among them. She will also rouse jealousy and envy among the women. The result is a breakdown in cooperation and team morale.

**32. Open the City Gates (and Pretend that All is Well).** When you're out-powered and outnumbered, feign nonchalance. Your opponent may misinterpret this to mean that you're more powerful than you appear.

**33. Sow Discord in the Enemy's Camp.** Plant rumors and seeds of discord among members of the opposing team. The internal strife will sap energy from their negotiation efforts.

**34. Inflict Injury on Yourself to Win the Enemy's Trust.** Pretending to be injured–pretending to have lost or failed–can make you appear less of a threat, attract sympathy, and let you get away with the devil.

**35. Use Several Strategies Simultaneously.** Combine tactics and don't rely on any one strategy at any one time. Use several strategies simultaneously and keep adapting them.

**36. If All Else Fails, Retreat.** If it's obvious you have no chance of winning, then retreat and regroup.

# APPENDIX VIII: KARAOKE: Your Folksong Repertoire

## Amazing Grace

*Chorus*

Amazing Grace, how sweet the sound,
That saved a wretch like me!
I once was lost but now am found,
Was blind but now I see.

'Twas grace that taught my heart to fear,
And grace my fears relieved.
How precious did that grace appear
The hour I first believed!

The Lord has promised good to me,
His word my hope secures.
He will my shield and portion be
As long as life endures.

Through many dangers, toils and snares,
I have already come;
'Tis grace has brought me safe thus far,
And grace will lead me home.

*Repeat Chorus*

## I've Been Working On The Railroad

I've been workin' on the railroad,
All the livelong day.
I've been workin' on the railroad,
Just to pass the time away.

Can't you hear the whistle blowing,
Rise up so early in the morn?
Can't you hear the captain shouting,
Dinah, blow your horn?

Dinah, won't you blow,
Dinah, won't you blow,
Dinah, won't you blow your horn?
Dinah, won't you blow,
Dinah, won't you blow,
Dinah, won't you blow your horn?

Someone's in the kitchen with Dinah.
Someone's in the kitchen I know.
Someone's in the kitchen with Dinah.
Strummin' on the old banjo, and singin':

Fe, fi, fiddly-i-o
Fe, fi, fiddly-i-o
Fe, fi, fiddly-i-o
Strummin' on the old banjo!

## My Bonnie Lies Over The Ocean

My Bonnie lies over the ocean,
My Bonnie lies over the sea,
My Bonnie lies over the ocean,
O bring back my Bonnie to me.

O blow ye winds over the ocean,
O blow ye winds over the sea,
O blow ye winds over the ocean,
And bring back my Bonnie to me!

*Chorus*
Bring back, bring back,
Bring back my Bonnie to me, to me,
Bring back, bring back,
O bring back my Bonnie to me!

Last night as I lay on my pillow,
Last night as I lay on my bed,
Last night as I lay on my pillow,
I dreamt that my Bonnie was dead.

The winds have blown over the ocean,
The winds have blown over the sea,
The winds have blown over the ocean,
And brought back my Bonnie to me.

*Repeat Chorus*

### Red River Valley

From this valley they say you are going.
We will miss your bright eyes and sweet smile.
For they say you are taking the sunshine,
That has brightened our path for a while.

*Chorus*

Come and sit by my side if you love me.
Do not hasten to bid me adieu.
But remember the Red River Valley
And the cowboy who loved you so true.

Won't you think of the valley you're leaving?
Oh how lonely, how sad it will be.
Oh think of the fond heart you're breaking,
And the grief you are causing to me.

*Repeat Chorus*

As you go to your home by the ocean,
May you never forget those sweet hours
That we spent in the Red River Valley,
And the love we exchanged mid the flow'rs.

*Repeat Chorus*

## Swing Low, Sweet Chariot

*Chorus*

Swing low, sweet chariot,
Comin' for to carry me home.
Swing low, sweet chariot,
Comin' for to carry me home.

I looked over Jordan and what did I see,
Comin' for to carry me home?
A band of angels comin' after me,
Comin' for to carry me home.

*Repeat Chorus*

If you get there before I do,
Comin' for to carry me home,
Tell all my friends I'm comin' too,
Comin' for to carry me home.

*Repeat Chorus*

The brightest day that ever I saw,
Comin' for to carry me home,
When Jesus washed my sins away,
Comin' for to carry me home.

*Repeat Chorus*

I'm sometimes up and sometimes down,
Comin' for to carry me home.
But still my soul feels heavenly bound,
Comin' for to carry me home.

# APPENDIX IX: Asian Resources

## Suggested Web Sites

The American Chamber of Commerce in Guangdong, www.amcham-guangdong.org.

Resource for promoting trade, commerce and investment between the U.S. and China. Links to useful resources in Guangdong and Pacific Rim.

Asia Pacific Management Forum, *Asian Business Strategy and Street Intelligence*

www.apmforum.com

Business strategy and research for success in Asian markets.

The Asian Wall Street Journal

www.awsj.com.hk

Paid subscription. Published in Hong Kong.

CFO Asia

www.cfoasia.com

Paid subscription magazine targeting financial directors in Asia. Covers topics from taxation to risk analysis and human resource management.

China Economic Review

www.chinaeconomicreview.com

English-language business news in China. Features stock market directory and investment analysis for China.

ChinaOnline

www.chinaonline.com

Portal site for links to weather, maps, telephone area codes, holidays, business news and weekly commentaries on China.

The Department of Foreign Affairs and International Trade, Government of Canada

www.voyage.gc.ca/consular_home-en.asp

Information about entry and visa requirements, traveling conditions and travel advisories for countries around the world.

The Economist, Country Briefings—China

www.economist.com/countries/China

Economic data, forecasts, articles and news briefs.

Expat Today, China

www.expat-today.com/china

Information on upcoming exhibitions and trade shows. Direct links to airlines that fly to China from major Western centers.

Hewitt Associates, Asia

www.hewittasia.com

HR company's publications include *Hewitt Quarterly, Asia Pacific and Hewitt Quarterly, China.*

Inside China Today

www.einnews.com/china

Provides access to news from world press sources, updated every 30 minutes.

Mandarin Tools

www.mandarintools.com/chinesename.html

Find out your name in Mandarin and your Chinese Zodiac. Includes Chinese/English dictionary and other language resources.

The United States Embassy in China

www.usembassy-china.org.cn

U.S. Commercial Services, China

www.buyusa.gov/china/en

Publishes *The China Commercial Brief* biweekly on various commercial sector developments in China. Also includes tips for doing business.

Xinhua News Agency

http://news.xinhuanet.com/english

Information on government, news and media (such as *Beijing Review* and *Shanghai Daily*), business, education and travel. Free access to statistics and white papers. Weather reports and current exchange rates.

Zhongwen.com

www.zhongwen.com

Learn about Chinese characters, history, literature and culture.

## Suggested Reading

### *Books*

Axtell, Roger E., ed. *Do's and Taboos Around the World: A Guide to International Behavior*. New York: John Wiley & Sons Inc., 1990.

Compilation of customs, protocol and laws for the international traveler. Includes cartoon-type illustrations of facial, hand, and arm gestures in countries around the globe.

Clissold, Tim. *Mr. China*. London: Robinson Books, 2004.

Compassionate accounting of the trials and tribulations and pitfalls that await anyone who expects to do business in China on Western terms. Based on the author's experiences as a partner of Jack Perkowski, the Wall Street Banker who founded Asimco in 1994.

DeMente, Boye Lafayette. *Japanese Etiquette & Ethics in Business* (6th edition). Chicago, Illinois: NTC Business Books, 1994.

Written by someone who has lived and worked in Japan for over twenty-five years, probes the apparently confusing and contradictory behavior of the Japanese businessperson.

Foster, Graham. *The Power of Positive Profit*. Nanjing, China: Everest Books, 2004

Makes the point that price management is the most neglected, yet most powerful tool for business success.

Funakawa, Atsushi. *Transcultural Management: A New Approach for Global Organizations*. San Francisco: Jossey-Bass Publishers, 1997.

A Japanese consultant presents a management model that addresses the challenges global firms face in managing in a multinational, multicultural and multilingual workplace.

Krippendorff, Kaihan. *The Art of the Advantage: 36 Strategies to Seize the Competitive Edge*. New York: Texere Publishing (a Thomson Learning US imprint), 2003.

How Microsoft, Sony, Coca-Cola, Virgin Airlines, and others "inadvertently" used Eastern business strategies to beat the competition.

Marsh, Robert M. *The Japanese Negotiator: Subtlety and Strategy Beyond Western Logic*. Tokyo: Kodansha International, 1988.

An expertly presented analysis of Japanese negotiating behavior and strategy of great help to Western negotiators.

Magee, David. *Turnaround: How Carlos Ghosn Rescued Nissan*. New York: Harper Information, 2003.

Tells how Ghosn's cross-cultural leadership style took Nissan from "strapped by $22-billion in debt, inflated supplier costs, and new product development that was at a standstill" to prominence and profitability within two years.

Morrison, Terri, Wayne A. Conaway, and George A. Borden, Ph.D. *Kiss, Bow or Shake Hands: How to Do Business in Sixty Countries*. Holbrooks, MA: Bob Adams, Inc., 1994.

Written by "executives who prepare other executives for international travel." Provides cultural overviews, behavior styles, negotiating techniques, protocol, and business practices in sixty countries.

Yuan, Gao. *Lure the Tiger Out of the Mountains: The Thirty-Six Stratagems of Ancient China*. New York: Simon & Schuster, 1991.

Subtitled "Timeless tactics from the East for today's successful manager," provides contemporary context for patterns of Chinese negotiating tactics designed to outwit the unsuspecting.

*Newspaper and Magazine Articles*

Beyond a Bail-Out, *The Economist*, 370, no. 8357 (January 10, 2004): 13.

Bulls in a China Shop. *The Economist*, 370, no. 8367 (March 20, 2004): 9-10.

A Survey of Business in China. *The Economist*, 370, no. 8367 (March 20, 2004): 3-19.

Graham, John L., and N. Mark Lam. The Chinese Negotiation. *Harvard Business Review* (October 2003): 82-91.

Craig S. Smith. Fearing Control by Microsoft, China Backs the Linux System. *The New York Times* (July 7, 2000).

*Scholarly Publications*

Malhotra, Deepak, and Keith J. Murnighan. The Effects of Contracts on Interpersonal Trust. *Administrative Science Quarterly* (Sept. 2002). Via FindArticles.com

http://www.findarticles.com/p/articles/mi_m4035/is_3_47/ai_97740703 (Accessed July 20, 2004).

An in-depth discussion of the effects of contracts on trust, as viewed through the lens of two laboratory experiments. Contains numerous reference texts that may be useful to HR personnel.

# APPENDIX X: Map of China

# APPENDIX XI:
# China History:
## A One-Minute History of a 4,000 to 5,000-Year-Old Culture, which Underscores the Reason Chinese Find it Difficult to Trust

### Internal Influences

China is one of the oldest nations in the world. Its recorded history dates back 5,000 years, during which time China has been inspired by religion (Confucianism, Taoism and Buddhism), ruled by a succession of dynasties, and torn by a long history of strife (military conflict, urban and commercial revolutions, internal chaos, civil war, warlords attempting to seize power, extermination campaigns, brutal crack-downs, genocide of the Tibetan culture, political reforms, economic restructurings, military dictatorships, civil rights abuses, official corruption, land redistribution, and intellectual oppression).

The Cultural Revolution (1966-70) closed universities, slaughtered intellectuals and caused widespread social unrest, culminating in the bloody Tiananmen Square massacre of student demonstrators in 1989. This was such an assault on traditional values that many who left China before the start of the Revolution are more Chinese in their cultural values than those who remained.

### External Influences

Foreigners have sought access to Chinese markets as far back as Marco Polo in the 13th century, in exchange for silk and tea. The effects of Britain's moves to rectify the trade imbalance by exporting opium to China in the 18th and 19th centuries resulted in the Opium War (also called the Anglo-Chinese War). China has never fully recovered from the humiliating defeat and ensuing separation into spheres of influence by Western powers. Hong Kong reverted to China in 1997, after 99 years of British rule. (Macao followed in 1999.)

### The Memories Remain

In brief, they have no reason to trust anyone. Although China's leaders have embraced free trade, the World Trade Organization accepted China in 2001, and China's first Olympic Games will be held in Beijing in 2008, the memories remain of a history of deception. The issue of trust is always there, ready to surface.

# ENDNOTES


1. Craig S. Smith, Fearing Control by Microsoft, China Backs the Linux System, *The New York Times* (July 7, 2000).

2. www.mandarintools.com. The subscription-based website includes tools for learning Mandarin, as well as free tools for finding your Mandarin name and Chinese Zodiac. Permission granted for mention by Erik Peterson.

3. *The Japan Times Ltd.*, March 16, 2003.

4. Quotation provided by Philip Revzin, *Asian Wall Street Journal* and *Far Eastern Economic Review*, in a press release issued September 5, 2001.

5. Reprinted with permission of Hewitt Associates LLC, a global HR outsourcing and consulting firm delivering a complete range of human capital management services. In 2001 and 2003, they conducted a survey of Chinese companies and CEOs to identify the top companies to work for in China. According to Hewitt, it all comes down to people issues.

6. Yang Jian, Senior Editor, "When Worlds Collide," *CFO China*, http://www.cfoasia.com/archives/200405-08.htm (accessed May 23, 2004).

7. Information for Appendix VI was generously provided during an interview with Kelvin Hutchinson, CEO, Vision in Action Pty Ltd. (Australia). Visit www.visioninaction.net.

8. Permission to copy "Suggested Working Paper Topics" granted. Extracted from "Systems for Success," a CD by Kelvin Hutchinson & David Julian Price. Phone: 0407 733 836 (Australia)

# ACKNOWLEDGMENTS

I am indebted to a number of individuals from Mainland China, Hong Kong, Taiwan, Japan, South Korea, Australia, Canada, and the United States, without whose gracious assistance this book would never have been written. In particular, Siemens VDO Automotive Inc. was the catalyst for the project, challenging me to prepare a seminar on doing business in Japan, then China and South Korea. They opened doors, made introductions, allowed me to interview their expatriate engineers, and introduced me to their joint venture partners in Asia, granting me constant access to an insider's viewpoint.

Special thanks to the Siemens team members across the globe who generously gave their time to talk about their experiences and insights: Roland Bauer, Vice President and General Manager, Motor Division (Germany); Xu Baoping, CEO, Siemens VDO Electric Motor (Shanghai) Co. Ltd., Yun Kim, Product Engineer, Business Development; JinSeung Lee, Applications Engineer, Motor Division; John Liang, P. Eng., Applications Engineer, Motor Division; Jun Lu, ME, P. Eng., Applications Engineer, Motor Division; André Veinotte, P. Eng., RD NAFTA Group. I am respecting the wishes of a few very helpful people who asked specifically not to be acknowledged in respect of their privacy.

I owe a special debt of gratitude to Joseph Varghese, Customer Projects Manager, Motor Division for his friendship and unflagging support, assistance and constant access to his team of engineers.

Thanks to Jon Aristone, Manager Marketing & Applications Engineering HVAC, for starting the whole process at Siemens with his enthusiastic endorsement of my communication training programs for engineers.

I am indebted to Yu-Hong (Beryl) Zhou, Polymer Specialist with Siemens (formerly with Dupont China), who was a major source of information for me on China.

Thanks to Calvin Wang, ME, Power Train Group, Engine Actuators & Emissions Management, Siemens VDO Automotive Inc., who tutored me on the fine points of Chinese business dealings.

Nate Iikubo, Advance Purchaser for a Japanese automotive Tier 1 firm (Detroit, Michigan, USA) generously shared his time and expertise on the concepts of *amae*, Asian trust and the inner circle, as well as the Japanese decision-making process.

I would also like to thank Brent D. Moorcroft, General Manager, Power Train Management Business Unit, Johnson Electric (Hong Kong) for his insider views as a Canadian expatriate working in Asia.

I sincerely thank Mr. Song Jong-Ho, Director Purchasing, Doowon Group (Seoul, Korea) for invaluable insights into his work as a JV partner.

Thanks also to Mark G. Maslen, B.A., D. Ac., who spent a year studying acupuncture in China and returned to North America with the lovely Yen Chung. Among other things, they provided the Mandarin translations in Appendix II.

Several colleagues and federation members of National Speakers Association (NSA) in America and Australia gave freely of their time and expertise, in the spirit of founder Cavett Roberts. Kelvin Hutchinson, APS, affectionately dubbed "serial entrepreneur" by his clients, spent eight successful years developing major businesses in China. He contributed the opening story in Secret #1 and provided the information in Appendix V: For the Entrepreneur: How to Find a Trusted Intermediary and Appendix VI: The Working Papers Way to Trust. Warren Evans, CSP, HoF challenged me to develop a model to explain the difference in how Asians and Westerners define trust. (The graphic appears in Secret #1.) I also thank Gerry Murak, Turnaround Performance Specialist, Murak & Associates, LLC for Million Dollar Mistake #4; Graham Foster, CSP, Director, Pacific Seminars International for his contribution to Secret #16; and Harold Wong, PhD, Berkeley University of California, for his insights.

Cover design and typography credits go to Fortunato Aglialoro. For the graphics, I am indebted to students Ben Perlman (map of China) and Wendy Zhu (chopsticks and restaurant seating).

Thank you to the divinely inspired Jane Girouard who worked with me on this project from conception to completion.

And, finally, thanks to my editor, Karen McRorie, for her willingness to ask the tough questions, helping me to shape and refine my thinking on each of the 17 Secrets. And to my son, Trevor Zelman, who patiently proofed and edited the final manuscript. Thanks also to my friend Iris Whitham, who taught me 25 years ago to drop every third word, and who considered it a privilege to read the final manuscript.

Although this writing represents the thoughts and cumulative experience of these many individuals, it does not follow that they will all agree with the way the information is presented in these pages. Any mistakes or omissions or misinterpretations are my own.

# ADVISORY PANEL
## China in Motion:
## Always in Motion and Up-to-Date

This book is a growing document. It is not the last word. It is only the last word to date. **CHINA IN MOTION** will be revised as new information is reported from the field from my Advisory Panel.

If you would like to become part of the group of advisors who keep me up-to-the-minute on current events in China, please contact me at advisor@chinainmotion.com. Your suggestions for corrections, additions and deletions are most welcome. If the information you share is used, you will be named in the acknowledgments, and you will receive a copy of the next edition of the book on publication.

# DISCLAIMER

# INDEX

## M



## N



## O



## P



## Q



## R

## S



## T



## U, V



## W



## X, Y, Z

# ABOUT THE AUTHOR

MIA DOUCET is owner, co-founder and Managing Director of Sales Development Institute (1993). She works with international blue chip organizations as a consultant, facilitator and coach. Her primary focus is increasing client profits through working with their people to stop making costly mistakes in China.

Prior to **CHINA IN MOTION**, Mia pioneered sales training techniques for an elite clientele of global giants in automotive and manufacturing technology firms. She worked to improve their engineers' contribution to corporate sales efforts through relationship building and effective communication.

Mia's unique ability to spark innovative and strategic thinking across whole divisions has made her a popular trainer across North America.

She belongs to several professional organizations and holds accreditations in education, sales and consulting. She is a Rotarian and a Paul Harris Fellow.

Mia is available to speak around the globe. She can be reached at mia@chinainmotion.com.

Bankerman Press

**CHINA IN MOTION**

# QUICK ORDER FORM

**Email orders:** orders@chinainmotion.com

**Telephone orders:** Call toll-free: 1-800-240-8734. Please have your credit card ready. If no one is available to take your call, leave a message and your order will be filled.

**Postal Orders:** Sales Development Institute, Picton Place, 22 Picton Street, Suite 1501, London, Ontario, Canada N6B 3R5.

Please send ____ copies of **China in Motion:**
***17 Secrets to Slashing the Time to Production, to Market, and to Profits in China, Japan and South Korea.***

*Please send more information on:*

☐ **Keynotes** ☐ **Seminars** ☐ **Consulting**

Name: ______________________________

Address: ______________________________

City: ______________________________

State: ________________ Zip: ________________

Email: ______________________________

Telephone: ______________________________

**Shipping:** *at cost*

**Payment:**

☐ International Postal Money Order ☐ Visa ☐ MasterCard

Card Number: ______________________________

Name on Card: ________________ Exp. Date: ______